Culture and Development

The Popular Theatre Approach in Africa

Penina Muhando Mlama

Nordiska Afrikainstitutet, Uppsala 1991
(The Scandinavian Institute of African Studies)

Indexing terms
Africa
Tanzania
Community development
Popular participation
Theatre

This book is published with support from SIDA (the Swedish International Development Authority)

Cover: Anna Bengtsson
Typesetting: Anne-Marie Vintersved
Editing: Kirsten Holst Petersen, Anna Rutherford and Mai Palmberg
Copyediting: Sonja Johansson

© Penina M Mlama and Nordiska Afrikainstitutet, 1991

Printed in Sweden by
Motala Grafiska, Motala 1991

ISBN 91-7106-317-X

Contents

Preface	5
1. Culture and development	7
2. Theatre and development	23
3. Popular theatre in Latin America and Asia	41
4. The background to popular theatre in Africa	55
5. The popular theatre movement in Africa from the 1970s	67
6. The theatre in Tanzania	97
7. Malya Popular Theatre Project 1982–1983	109
Objectives of the project	109
The background of Malya village	110
Research and problem analysis	111
The theatre process	115
Post-performance discussion with the audience	118
Follow-up action	120
The animateur team's third visit	123
The animateur team's fourth visit	128
The animateur team's fifth visit	130
8. Bagamoyo Popular Theatre Workshop 1983	139
Background to Bagamoyo	139
Research and information gathering	141
Finding out the problems of the people	142
The theatre performance process	143
Post-performance discussion	153
Follow-up action	155
9. Msoga Popular Theatre Workshop 1985	157
Background to Msoga	157
The Msoga performances	159
Information gathering	160
The popular theatre performance	163
The Bigililo group's performance	164
Post-performance discussion	172

Follow-up action	174
10. Mkambalani Popular Theatre Workshop 1986	177
Background to Mkambalani	177
Research and problem analysis	179
The theatre process	185
Gombesugu	186
Nzekule	188
Kipuku	192
Mkwajungoma (Zembwela group)	194
Post-performance discussion with the audience	198
Follow-up action	200
Conclusion	203
Bibliography	213

Preface

The reflections in this book are a result of a decade's theoretical and practical preoccupation with Popular Theatre in relation to development.

The Popular Theatre movement in Africa is a response to a history that has undermined people's genuine participation in the development process. Development strategies in Africa have often disregarded the grassroot view and given little consideration to the incorporation of development action into the way of life of the communities concerned. By neglecting the peoples' cultures this approach to development has also led to a disregard of local communication processes through aspirations for development.

This book reviews the relation between culture and development focusing on Popular Theatre as a specific approach towards incorporating a people's view on development.

The reflections in this book derive from the author's practical participation in Popular Theatre workshops in various villages in Tanzania, Bangladesh, Zimbabwe and Cameroon. During these workshops several weeks were spent in grassroot communities. The Popular Theatre process involved the participation of amateurs and the whole community in researching into what the community felt were their development problems. An analysis of the problems was done through individual and group discussions. The problems were then concretised into theoretical performances by the members of the community, using artistic forms familiar to the community. A public performance was staged to present the problems and suggestions for solutions. A post-performance discussion by the performers and audience charted out what action to be taken by the community to solve the problems raised.

Included in this book are the Popular Theatre experiences up to 1988 when this book was written. There have been further developments especially in giving quality to the process with view to maximising the participation potential of the communities involved. More development agents are now adopting this approach having recognised its effectiveness.

The production of this book would not have been possible without the assistance of many people. It is not possible to mention everyone by name especially considering that whole villages were involved in the workshops. However, my sincere appreciation goes first to the members of the villages in which I worked namely: Malya, Msoga, Bagamoyo, Mkambalani in Tanzania, Murewa in Zimbabwe, and Konye in Cameroon. It is from these people that I learnt the meaning of development.

Popular Theatre work is basically team work and many thanks go to the team of animateurs with whom I worked in all the workshops. I make special mention of Amandina Lihamba with whom I have conducted most of the Popular Theatre work in Tanzania.

For the work outside Tanzania I was greatly assisted by the International Popular Theatre Alliance and especially Ross Kidd on whose practical and theoretical work I have made many references. Ross Kidd has also made a great contribution in inspiring the Popular Theatre work in Africa. The Union of African Performing Artists also deserves mention for its stand on supporting Popular Theatre work.

The theoretical reflections on this work was facilitated by a very generous moral and financial support from the Rockefeller Foundation through an award on Reflections and Development, the Swedish Institute, the Swedish International Development Authority, the Scandinavian Institute of African Studies and the University of Dar es Salaam.

Finally I am greatly indebted to my family: my husband Raphael, my daughter Mota, and my son Huila who have patiently stood by me in a decade of work that has frequently taken me away from them.

Penina Muhando Mlama
Dar es Salaam
1991

CHAPTER 1
Culture and development

The 1980s have witnessed an interesting debate arising from a realisation of an apparent failure of previous development strategies to better the lives of the majority of the world population. Referring to the rural poor of the developing countries, Khan and Bhasin observe that "the development strategies and programmes implemented during the last three decades have failed to attack the causes of rural poverty. The benefits of whatever development growth has taken place have not trickled down. Landlessness has increased and so have poverty, unemployment and inequality. Peasants, landless people, plantation workers and women have been marginalised. In addition to this, through environmental destruction, the very resource base of the people is being rapidly destroyed."[1]

Many reasons have been advanced to explain this state of affairs. The global and national unequal distribution of capital and wealth is one. In spite of attempts to achieve a more equal partnership for developing countries in the trade and financial systems, international terms of exchange continue to negatively affect the living standards of the majority in those countries.[2] At the national level, the division of the gross national production remains a source of internal tensions with a few amassing wealth and privileges at the expense of the majority. The concentration of industry, technology and finance in a few countries of the North has created dependent economies for all the poor countries. Even though the North is dependent on the Third World for energy and

---

1. Khan, N. and K. Bhasin 1986, "Sharing one earth", Asian South Pacific Bureau of Adult Education, *Courier Service*, No. 37.
2. See AAWORD "The Dakar Declaration on Another Development with Women", *Development Dialogue* 1–2, 1982, The Dag Hammarskjöld Foundation, Uppsala.

raw materials, its economic and military powers give it a strong grip on the welfare of the Third World.[1]

Other reasons have included faulty, inappropriate and incompetent planning marring most Third World development strategies. For example, the top-down development planning that denies the broad masses popular participation in the determination of their political, economic and social welfare has led to the failure of many development projects. Lack of technologically skilled personnel, overpopulation, natural disasters, illiteracy, corruption are but a few of the other reasons.

The neglect of culture or the non-recognition of culture as an integral component of the development process is another factor that has gained much prominence in the debate.

Attention is increasingly drawn to the fact that development strategies have over-emphasised economic growth at the expense of the social and cultural factors which are just as crucial to the well-being of a people. "To date, economists have in general, focused on structural changes such as increased financial opportunities and incentives, assuming that externally defined rational reactions to such interventions would result in appropriate behavioural change for development."[2] To facilitate the structural changes in the developing countries, the prescription has always been economic and technical assistance from the reservoirs of advanced science and technology of the developed countries. For many years, Third World development has been seen as simply a transfer in health, agriculture and education. Development planning, therefore, became the preserve of economic planners and technical experts together with their local and foreign political masters and benefactors. Economic and technical considerations have been the force behind the choice of introduction and distribution of development projects over and above social-cultural gains.

Many arguments have been advanced calling for the need to look at culture as a necessary component of development. Swantz

---

1. See Abdalla, I., "Heterogeneity and Differentiation, The End of the Third World?", *Development Dialogue* 2, 1982, The Dag Hammarskjöld Foundation, Uppsala.
2. Colleta, N. and R. Kidd eds. 1980, Tradition and Development, (German Foundation for Development, Berlin).

argues that "not only a mentality of trust in one's own cultural heritage, but also a deep understanding of different cultural patterns and ways of perceiving and conceptualising practical life situations is crucial for development in general".[1]

The UNESCO suggestion to the United Nations for a Decade for Cultural Development in 1983 is an indication of the importance now accorded to culture and development. Since then UNESCO has organised a number of meetings on the cultural dimension of development including one in The Hague and another one in Helsinki, both in 1985.[2] The Helsinki meeting had as its objectives to gather theoretical and practical knowledge on the cultural dimension of development, to call the attention of authorities responsible for development projects to the importance of this cultural dimension, and to develop new thinking and ideas on the subject.[3] Suggestions emanating from these meetings on how to implement the integration of culture in development include the involvement of anthropologists in the formulation, implementation and evaluation of development projects, the setting up of financial support for cultural identities and the preservation of monuments and other cultural heritages. One also sees that development agents and financial institutions are much more willing now than ten years ago to support projects and programmes with a cultural bearing.

Following the debate on culture and development, however, it is obvious that there is no consensus on how to go about addressing this issue. Nieuwenhuijze points out that there may even be contradictory conceptions of culture and development. He argues that "the current interest in culture and development is largely a western response, under a typically western label, to Third World events not necessarily announced there as cultural. They may occasionally be featured as socio-cultural, or they may, notably in the Islamic world, be announced as religious or they may even be disguised as political". In western parlance, then the label "cultural" serves as a catch-all indication of matters sensed rather

---

1. Swantz, Marja-Liisa ed. 1985, *The Cultural Dimension of Development*, Finnish National Commission for UNESCO, Helsinki.
2. See *The Cultural Dimension of Development* 1985.
3. Swantz ed., *op. cit.*

than identified, apprehended rather than understood. "In the Third World, on the other hand", Nieuwenhuijze argues "culture and development relates back to the liberation urge of late colonial days, the urge to reassert identity, collective and perhaps individual too, which was part of Nationalism." Nationalism was taken to be mainly political "but it seems", he continues, "that it was in fact the tip of a cultural iceberg".[1] Other views have also been expressed that "culture and development" is probably a passing fad like "rural development", "integrated development" and many others before it.

Undoubtedly, much of the confusion and the inability of the advocates of culture and development to come up with a specific agenda on what action to take results from a lack of a clear definition of culture.

Culture is a term that has so far eluded definition. It is not the intention here to delve into the debate on what culture is. Suffice it to say that culture here refers to a people's way of life, a way of perceiving and doing things that identifies one people as distinct from another. A culture derives its qualities from the conditions—economic, political and social—existing in a society. But at the same time a culture determines the regeneration of these conditions.

A feudal society, for example, is bound to produce a feudalist culture in which a few people perceive themselves and act in a way that suggests they have the right to own all the land and to subject the rest of the people to a life of serfdom. The serfs, on the other hand, perceive themselves as inferior to the landlord and accept it as God-given that they should give away most of the fruit of their labour to the landlord. Many ideological tools are used, including religion, education, language and the arts, to consolidate this way of life, as a result of which people continue to perceive and do things as landlords or as serfs and thus keep the feudal structure intact. This is true for any other mode of production. Culture is, therefore, at the same time a reflection and a determinant of the workings of a society's structures.

---

1. Nieuwenhuijze, C. van 1983, *Culture and Development, The Prospects of an After-Thought*, Institute of Social Studies, Occasional Papers No. 97, The Hague.

To effect change in the basic structure of a society, therefore, means changing a people's way of life, a people's way of perceiving and doing things to support the intended changes. Indeed, history has seen many societies evolving different cultures to support successive but different modes of production. The colonised societies in Africa, for example, had a colonial-cum-capitalist culture imposed on them that made them look upon the coloniser as some sort of god and thus facilitate political, economic, and social subjugation vital to the colonisation process. The introduction of socialism has also often been accompanied by efforts not only to build a socialist economy but also a socialist culture to support it. The Chinese Cultural Revolution of the 1960s is an obvious example. At every stage of a society's existence, there is a culture to support its structures.

The question then is why the concept of "Development" applied to the developing countries in the last three decades assumes that societal structural change could come about purely based on economic factors. How could development experts remain indifferent to the inseparable relationship between economic and cultural factors?

One explanation could be sheer ignorance on the part of development planners and agents and their inability to learn from the many examples of history. Such ignorance is, indeed, very unfortunate—even more so considering that most of these people are supposedly intellectuals. It seems more logical, therefore, to assume that the neglect of the cultural dimension of development in the developing countries is by design rather than ignorance. Development, as it has been applied to Africa, Asia and Latin America, is actually another name for capitalism. Development strategies, especially those designed externally, have been, in reality, different means to facilitate the penetration of capitalism in the "underdeveloped" or "undercapitalist" countries. And there has been at the same time, a corresponding capitalist culture to support the capitalist structures. What has been neglected is not culture as such but rather specific cultures incompatible with the entrenchment of capitalism.

Since the introduction of capitalism in Asia, Africa and Latin America, a capitalist culture has been promoted. Various cultural tools, including religion, education, language, and the arts, have been used effectively to promote a capitalist way of life. In Africa, for example, the introduction of capitalist culture goes back to colonialism which was one of capitalism's effective arms. Educational systems were introduced to produce a small African elite with values and attitudes that made them look upon themselves as superior to the illiterate majority and aspire to be like the colonial masters whom they then assisted to maintain colonialism and thus facilitate the continual exploitation of their countries.

Today, long after the colonial master has left, this elite is still bowing to the white man, faithfully guarding his capitalist interests, and sometimes selling whole nations' resources to foreign interests and even allowing various forms of military occupation to thwart any possible attempts by the people to free themselves from the claws of capitalism. As Ngugi observes, "the freedom for western finance capital and for the vast transnational monopolies under its umbrella to continue stealing from the countries and peoples of Latin America, Africa, Asia and Polynesia is today protected by conventional and nuclear weapons. Imperialism presents the struggling peoples of the earth and all those calling for peace, democracy and socialism with the ultimatum: accept theft or death".[1]

Colonialism also used the Christian religion to drive the masses into a culture of silence, accepting colonialism and its accompanying capitalist exploitation as God-given and compromising their poverty and humiliation with a promise for the kingdom of heaven. Good Christians were expected to stay out of politics that would question the workings of colonialism, and many liberation movements faced stiff opposition from their fellow countrymen who, as Christians, were made to believe that fighting for their independence was the work of the devil. Analysing the position of the churches in Kenya for and against the Mau Mau movement, for example, Chepkwony[2] observes that "the churches and particularly the revival of Christians were deeply involved in the detention camps with rehabilitation and repentance of ex-freedom

---

1. Ngugi wa Thiong'o 1986, *Decolonising the Mind,* James Currey, London.
2. Chepkwony, Agnes 1987, *The Role of Non-governmental Organisations in Development: A Study of the National Christian Council of Kenya (NCCK) 1963–1978,* Uppsala.

fighters in order to make them denounce their contacts. In this situation of conflict, many revival Christians became pacifists".

Even though many churches today are taking an active part in development projects, the majority of Christians in Africa are, in the name of Christianity, incapable of radically challenging the exploitative and oppressive forces in their societies. Probably the greatest conflict of the church in Africa today, is what role it should play in the struggles of its followers against capitalist forces.

The position of the church in South Africa's apartheid regime is a striking example. The Kairos document, a theological comment on the political crisis in South Africa and a critique of current theological models in the country observes that:

> When we also come to see that the conflict in South Africa is between the oppressor and the oppressed, the crisis for the church as an institution becomes much more acute. Both the oppressor and the oppressed claim loyalty to the same church ... There we sit in the same church while outside Christian policemen and soldiers are beating up and killing Christian children and torturing Christian prisoners to death while yet other Christians stand by and weakly plead for peace.[1]

Similarly, the arts have been an effective tool for capitalist culture. With the theatre, for instance, Africa saw the introduction of British and French theatre with the intention of inculcating European artistic values in the subjects.[2] Although Europe had seen many working class theatre movements that were part of the European peoples' struggles against the evils of capitalism, the theatre introduced to Africa was bourgeois, refusing to address itself to the realities of the overall socio-economic conditions of the societies concerned. Because it was the theatre of that class which could afford "art for art's sake", it is not surprising that the European theatre directors of the colonial times could, without shame, stage plays in Africa that were totally irrelevant to the realities of the lives of the African people. The colonial subjects who participated

---

1. *The Kairos Document, Challenge to the Church. A Theological Comment on the Political Crisis in South Africa,* Braamfontein 1986.
2. On this subject see E. Hussein 1975, *The Development of Drama in East Africa,* Ph.D. thesis, Humboldt University, Berlin; Penina Mlama 1983, *Tanzanian Traditional Theatre as a Pedagogical Institution,* Ph.D. thesis, University of Dar es Salaam; Ngugi wa Thiong'o, *op. cit.*

in this theatre, however, came to understand theatre, and indeed, the arts as a whole, as mere entertainment, a pastime, something divorced from the serious concerns of life. They were not aware of the fact that this "art for art's sake" was designed to enhance capitalist structures. It was a deliberate effort to paralyse the ability of the arts to question injustice and to create awareness that could move people to fight against colonialism. To benefit capitalism art needed to be purely aesthetic, "art" only and not "politics".

When after independence this African elite formed the ruling class and stepped into the shoes of the colonial masters to guard capitalist interests in their countries, they continued to support an art for art's sake theatre in order to maintain the status quo. It is interesting to note that even those countries which used the arts to mobilise people to support the independence struggles and, therefore, saw the effectiveness of the arts as a mobilisation and consciousness raising tool, have resorted again to art for art's sake.

Huynh argues that "national liberation movements use ideologically determined national characteristics in order to provide stronger legitimation for the national struggle, to extend their own socio-cultural sphere of influence to the detriment of foreign elements, and thus conduct their campaign more effectively. But once national independence is achieved, this tactical strategy is relegated to the background".[1]

Governments have been content to patronise only that theatre which will not question the exploitative and oppressive structures characterising most of independent Africa. And generally they have taken a position that see the arts as a luxury which the new nations cannot afford. But in truth, this is meant to mask the potential of the arts to challenge the corruption and injustices of the ruling classes. This explains why even though the governments argue that the arts are a luxury, they have always found the resources with which to maintain active censorship boards and other systems to keep the arts that depart from the art for art's sake function in check. Indeed, governments have not been slow in repressing radical theatre practices. The Kamiriithu theatre experience discussed in chapter 5 is just one example.

---

1. Huynh, C. 1981, *Cultural Identity and Development*, Reports/Studies, UNESCO, Paris.

Some regimes have adopted an approach of co-opting the arts and thus ensuring that they are on the side of the ruling class, propagating its ideology and mobilising the people to maintain the status quo. In the guise of promoting national cultural identities, the arts have been turned into political mouthpieces of government or party policies, exhorting people to abide by government plans and to be grateful to the leaders for their independence and whatever development has come their way. The airport or state banquet dances fashionable with many African countries is one manifestation of such art.

As such, the majority of ruling classes in Africa have maintained an artistic practice that facilitates the continuation of neo-colonial structures and the deeper penetration of capitalist forces. The multinationally controlled electronic media consolidates this situation by making available capitalist value-loaded cultural tools such as films, books, pop music, television and video programmes which create in the African people a taste for a way of life compatible with capitalist interests.

A variety of cultural tools are operating in Africa imposing and developing a capitalist culture vital to the entrenchment of capitalism. The development of capitalism, therefore, has been supported by a consciously designed development of a supporting capitalist culture. To imagine that the agents of capitalism would attempt to penetrate Africa without developing a cultural system to support the system is to underrate the powers of capitalism.

Development strategies which, as mentioned earlier, are basically designed to consolidate capitalism and imperialism in the developing countries, have not neglected culture. As Amilcar Cabral observes:

> The practice of imperialist rule demands a more or less accurate knowledge of the society it rules and of the historical reality, both economic, social and cultural, in the middle of which it exists. In fact, man has never shown as much interest in knowing other men and other societies as during this century of imperialist domination. An unprecedented mass of information, of hypotheses and theories has been built up, notably in the fields of history, ethnology, ethnography, sociology and culture concerning peoples or groups brought under imperialist domination.[1]

---

1. Cabral, Amilcar 1973, *Return to the Source: Selected Speeches*, Africa Information Service, New York.

This information has played a vital role by providing capitalism with a guide to facilitate cultural conditions to support the capitalist system. While colonialism tried without too much success to forcefully suppress and eliminate the cultures of the subject people, development strategies have adopted more subtle approaches.

First is the pretense that indigenous cultures do not exist or that they are of no consequence to the development of a people. African governments are, therefore, led to believe that the development of their countries will be achieved only through economic plans and a transfer of technical knowledge from the developed countries. Whatever this does to a people's way of life is supposed to be development. Clashes between this economic or technological imposition and the indigenous cultures have led to the accusation that culture impedes development. Indeed, indigenous cultures have often been labelled backward and anti-development. The assumption is that any society wishing to develop needs to discard its indigenous cultures. This is what Ngugi refers to as a "cultural bomb":

> ... the biggest weapon wielded and actually daily unleashed by imperialism ... (and intended) to annihilate a people's belief in their names, in their languages, in their environment, in their heritage of struggle, in their unity, in their capacities and ultimately in themselves. It makes them see their past as one wasteland of non-achievement and it makes them want to distance themselves from that wasteland.[1]

In the place of the indigenous cultures, development strategies have led the African governments into adopting a conception of culture limited to museums, libraries, handicrafts, sports, and the arts. Ministries of culture have been established with responsibilities limited to this narrow conception of culture. In fact there is so much confusion over what culture is that most of these culture ministries have not managed to produce clear-cut policies or guidelines. African countries are characterised by an absence of cultural policies.

The UNESCO-sponsored publications on cultural policy in different countries displayed the confusion about the meaning of

---

1. Ngugi wa Thiong'o 1986.

culture.[1] National budgets or development plans give very low priority to culture since it is only presented as football or traditional dances and handicrafts as opposed to the supposedly more serious concerns like industry, agriculture or health. This is illustrated by budget allocations in Tanzania. Culture is paraded as something that people can do without, something not worth much attention. And in line with the capitalist concept of culture, it is separate from economics or politics. It exists as a pastime, something people engage in when they have nothing serious to do.

This negation of indigenous non-capitalist cultures and the adoption of the capitalist concept of culture has created a fertile ground for the penetration of capitalism. Development strategies have been instrumental in bringing about this state of affairs. What is seen therefore, is not the neglect of the cultural dimension of development but rather a consolidation of capitalism with its corresponding culture. Today, more than ever before, people in Africa are confused about their identity. They have lost the power to perceive themselves as an entity and to recognise the good and the bad forces for their general welfare. They have lost the ideological tools with which to challenge the exploitative forces' encroachment over their way of life. They are confusing the capitalist way of life with modernity, exploitation with social success, repression with political power, and so on. No nation's culture is strong enough to pose as a challenge to the increasing dominance of capitalism.

Naturally, due to this success of capitalism, development has not been forthcoming to the majority of the world population. People have become poorer, the quality of life has worsened and more and more people cannot even produce enough to feed themselves. Millions are starving to death. The few who have amassed wealth at the expense of others, often resort to repressive measures, silencing the majority into an acceptance of their exploitation. The majority are excluded from participating in policy making or planning their own development. They are instead only expected to implement programmes formulated by others, even when such programmes are not for the benefit of the common

---

1. See UNESCO 1974, *Studies and Documents on Cultural Policies*, UNESCO Press, Paris.

man and woman. Rarely are they given the chance to question the unfair returns for their labour. There is little or no dialogue between those in power and the ruled. In the name of development, charity or aid, foreign technology is imposed on rural areas with little consideration for its impact on the recipients' way of life. Indeed, little attention is paid to what the majority think, feel or want. Theirs is supposed to be a culture of silence, an uncritical acceptance of the status quo.

But the exploited masses of Africa have not always accepted this culture of silence. They have evolved a culture of resistance in order to fight the forces of their exploitation and oppression. It is this culture of resistance which previously enabled some of them to take up arms and fight colonial domination. It is this culture of resistance that now sometimes sporadically flares into clashes between the masses and the ruling classes as manifested, for example, in the demonstrations against the increase in food prices in the early 1980s in Zambia and Sudan. At other times this resistance has culminated in mass demonstrations in blind support for military coup d'états that promise redemption from exploitation even though such regimes have yet to deliver the goods. It is this culture of resistance that has been the driving force behind peasants refusing to adopt new techniques or practices in agriculture, health, education and the like.

It is this culture of the dominated classes, the culture of resistance against exploitation and oppression, that the development strategies have ignored. It is this culture that needs to be an integral part of any development strategy that is genuinely concerned with the need to better the lives of the majority. It is this culture that will enable the majority to mobilise themselves against the exploitative forces whose elimination is an inevitable prerequisite to their authentic development. It is this culture that needs to be promoted and fostered as a necessary step towards the development of the majority of the African people which has so far eluded most development strategies.

The problem of development today, therefore, is not the integration of just any culture but rather the culture of the exploited majority. An argument could here be advanced that the only logical way to bring about development is to uproot capitalism. It is true that no elimination of the exploitation of the majority is possible within a capitalist structure. It is with this realisation that some African countries like Tanzania, Zimbabwe, Guinea, Mozambique and others have embarked on a socialist path. However, one of the factors that has contributed to the apparent difficulties in realising the socialist goals in these countries is a failure to cultivate a culture of the majority.

The leaders of most socialist-oriented countries have imposed the ideas of the ruling classes on the people. Although in theory the people are supposed to determine their lives and to democratically participate in decision-making and planning of their welfare, practice has leaned towards inhibiting bureaucracies and at times even dictatorial leadership.

Nor are leaders in socialist-oriented countries any clearer about what culture is or its relationship with the socio-economic structures. For example, the Arusha Declaration, the blueprint of Tanzania's *Ujamaa* (socialism) omits any reference to culture and socialism.[1]

In most cases culture has been seen merely as the use of the cultural tools, especially the arts, to propagate socialist ideology as stipulated by the ruling class. Culture is often regarded as synonymous with political propaganda. Whereas the majority of the people in these countries may not be as economically exploited as those in capitalist-oriented countries, they are just as excluded from determining what is best for their livelihood. Worse still, those in power are often amassing wealth and privileges through exploiting the resources that are supposed to be shared by all. The inability of these states to free themselves from the global market structures that are inherently capitalist has subjected the peasants and workers to the same exploitative and oppressive forces as elsewhere. The majority of the people in these countries also need to promote their culture of resistance to struggle against both local and foreign forces in the attempt to attain genuine socialism.

The challenge to development strategies, therefore, is not only to bring about economic growth but also to evolve a culture that will support the conditions necessary to such growth and enable the betterment of the life of all sectors of the population.

---

1. See J. Nyerere 1968, *Freedom and Socialism*, Oxford University Press.

It ought to be noted here that some efforts towards this goal have been going on, using different cultural tools to integrate the political, social, and economic factors in trying to improve the quality of life. Education, for example, has seen attempts to use knowledge as a liberating process. Adult education, especially Paulo Freire's approach, has provided literacy skills as a means through which people could analyse their situations and take action to solve problems impeding their development. The mass media, on the other hand, has also seen some attempts to democratise communication through the use of media more widely accessible to the grassroots.[1]

The theatre in Africa has also produced attempts towards a wider participation of people in determining their way of life. This study traces the relationship between theatre and development. It deals, however, especially with the popular theatre movement in Africa which has been a conscious attempt not only to bring to the fore the voice of the dominated classes but also to involve them in the process of bettering their way of life. In Popular Theatre, people research into their problems of life, discuss and analyse them, bringing out their root causes and suggesting their possible solutions. The problems are also concretised in theatrical portrayals incorporating the people's viewpoints and expressions, followed by collective strategising and mobilisation for action to solve the problems in question.

Chapter 2 introduces the relationship between theatre in general and development showing that throughout history, there has been a close relationship between theatre and a people's welfare. As an ideological tool the theatre has been used to discuss issues, to educate, to create awareness and often to mobilise people for specific action including liberation struggles.

Chapter 3 narrows the focus to Popular Theatre, first giving an overview of Popular Theatre in Latin America and Asia to demonstrate parallels with the Popular Theatre movement in Africa. Popular Theatre as a process, has seen common application among oppressed people all over the world. Specific examples are given from the Philippines, Nicaragua, India, and Bangladesh.

---

1. See Worldview Information Foundation 1986, Report 1980/1986, Colombo.

Chapter 4 provides a general background to the emergence of Popular Theatre in Africa. The major argument is that Popular Theatre has always existed in Africa as the theatre of the dominated classes, who have used it to fight various oppressive forces including feudal and colonial powers. The problem has been that the dominant classes have either ignored or suppressed this type of theatre and patronised instead those theatre forms that safeguarded their won interests. An overview of such theatre before the 1970s is presented.

Chapter 5 traces the Popular Theatre movement in Africa from the 1970s to the present. The major approaches in the movement from Southern, East and West Africa are included showing the developments in techniques and ideological outlooks over the years. The shortcomings and strengths of the various models are brought out through the discussion of specific examples of Popular Theatre undertakings.

Chapter 6 to 10, are devoted entirely to Popular Theatre in Tanzania. This part begins with an introduction to the Tanzanian theatre scene giving the context from which the Popular Theatre movement has emerged. Four specific cases of Popular Theatre programmes are presented with some detailed description of the process in terms of the different stages; the theatrical process and the discussions and follow-up action that was involved in each programme.

The Popular Theatre movement in Africa in relation to the question of culture and development is discussed in the concluding section. Various cases presented in the study are assessed, and the conclusion is drawn that Popular Theatre does present one concrete example of an attempt to treat culture as inseparable from development.

CHAPTER 2
Theatre and development

Raised eyebrows are a frequent reaction to the mentioning of theatre in discussions related to development. It is difficult for many development agents to visualise theatre as having any relation to development. This reflects a general negative view of theatre in many parts of the world. Reviewing the attitudes towards theatre in Europe, Whiting observes that in many cases the value and potentials of theatre have been disregarded:

> To the Romans, theatre was little more than a degraded pleasure, a project by slaves for the titillation of their masters. To the early church, theatre was an evil to be crushed, along with thievery and prostitution. To many entertainers, such as strolling players and television comedians, theatre has been regarded as a means of earning a living through a few jokes and antics to catch the momentary fancy of the general public. To some parents, the theatre is an evil bound to wreck the personality of a child who succumbs to its lures.[1]

Such attitudes towards theatre derive from capitalist cultural conceptions that have, indeed, produced theatre forms whose main function is to entertain. The mainstream theatre in America and Europe as well as much of the urban theatre in developing countries fit this description. Because of capitalist conditions, theatre has been turned into a commodity which must emphasise its most purchasable elements in order to be saleable.

Although entertainment is an essential component of any theatre worth the name, to restrict the essence of theatre to entertainment is most unfortunate. History has seen numerous examples of other functions of theatre and this has been noted by various scholars. Louis Harrap maintain that the major function of the arts (including theatre) is to shape people's consciousness. Treating in detail the evolution of the arts, he states that art has operated as a social force because it contributes to the shaping of con-

---

1. Whiting, F. 1954, *An Introduction to the Theatre*, Harper & Row Publishers, New York.

sciousness and has played a part in moving people to social action. He argues that art is a form of persuasion and hence has the power to modify conscience and to influence belief. The persuasive effect of art is maximised when the audience responds to its value or is compelled to accept the feelings, ideas and characters portrayed. The work of art tends to influence its audience to active acceptance or rejection. The audience internalises the various experiences conveyed, which in turn modify consciousness and existing attitudes.[1]

The ability of the arts to shape a people's consciousness is what leads to the view, popular especially in socialist countries like China or Russia, that sees the function of the arts and literature as basically ideological with great potential to effect the success of revolutionary processes in a society. The arts are seen as a necessary component of the struggle towards attaining socialist ideals. Art and literature are perceived as playing a role, equal to that of economics, politics and the military in the revolutionary struggle. This view is reflected in Mao's famous address to the Chinese artists at the Yenan Forum where he says:

> Revolutionary art and literature are part of the entire cause of the revolution, they are its cogs and screw, indispensable to the whole machine, and form an indispensable part of the entire cause of the revolution. If we had no art and literature even in the broadest and most general sense, then the revolutionary movement could not be carried to victory.[2]

The Cuban Escambry Theatre and the peasant theatre movement organised by MECATE in Nicaragua are specific examples of the use of theatre for revolutionary purposes.[3]

A more accepted and equally ideological—though not always revolutionary—function of theatre is that linked to education. Great thinkers have acknowledged the close association of theatrical elements (play, imitation and creativity) and learning. Aristotle, to whom imitation is central to theatre, says:

---

1. See Harrap, L. 1949, *The Social Roots of the Arts*, International Publishers, New York.
2. Mao Tse-tung, 1956 "Talks at the Yenan Forum on Art and Literature", *Selected Works*, International Publishers, New York.
3. See Bustos, N. 1982, "Interview with Nidia Bustos", *Theaterwork Magazine*, House of Print, Minnesota, Vol. 2, No. 6.

Imitation is natural to man from childhood, one of his advantages over the lower animals being this, that he is the most imitative creature in the world and learns first by imitation.[1]

Plato believed that education must be based upon play and not compulsion and that "children from their earliest years must take part in all the more lawful forms of play, for if they are not surrounded with such an atmosphere they can never grow up to be well educated and virtuous citizens".[2] And Horace argues that "a poet gets every vote who unites information with pleasure, at once enlightening and instructing the reader".[3]

In his book *Play, Drama and Thought, the Intellectual Background to Education*, Richard Courtney discusses the use of theatre, drama in particular, in different historical eras. Athenian education in the 5th century BC was based on literature which included reading, writing and recitations from Greek dramatists. Greek theatre was a great educational instrument because it disseminated knowledge and was, for the populace, the only literary pleasure available.

In spite of the sharp conflict between theatre and the medieval church due to the church's resentment of the theatre's satirical treatment of the church and the theatre's presence also in pagan rites, liturgical drama became a very forceful didactic movement. It emerged following the church's own recognition of the capacity to help the illiterate to comprehend the faith. From the 9th century and "for five centuries the mystery and morality plays provided the only intellectual pleasure for the multitudes. Schools and books, after all, were the prerogative of the few. It was drama that provided the masses with what education they had".[4]

By the 16th century, dramatic activities took place in many schools in Europe. The Vittario de Feltra Academy in Italy and Saint Cyr Convent for girls in France are examples of schools that gave prominence to learning through theatrical activities.

---

1. Aristotle, *Poetics*, Pitman Sons, 1927, London.
2. Plato, *The Republic*, (trans. A.D. Lindsay), Everyman, 1935, London.
3. Horace, F., *Art of Poetry*, (trans. T. Moxon), Everyman, 1934, London.
4. Courtney, R. 1968, *Play, Drama and Thought, the Intellectual Background to Drama in Education*, Drama Book Specialists, New York.

Prominent educationalists in Europe and America have recognised the importance of "play" to education. Rousseau, later supported by Pestalozzi, advocated that a child's early education should consist almost entirely of play, an idea that inspired Basedow to start a school—The Philathropium—in Hamburg, where work and play were to be synonymous.[1] John Dewey's famous theory, "learning by doing", highlighted further the place of creative play in education.

> The primary root of all educative activity is the instructive, impulsive attitudes and activities of the child and not in the presentation and application of external material, whether through the ideas of others or through the senses: and that accordingly, numberless spontaneous activities of children, plays, games, mimic effort ... are capable of educational use, and are the foundation stone of educational method.[2]

Such thinking gave rise to strong 20th century movements which have sought to demonstrate in practice the place and role of theatre in formal education. Famous among these is the British Cook's "The play way" methodology based on the principle that proficiency and learning come not from reading and listening but from action, from doing, from experience. Good work, Cook notes, is more often the result of spontaneous effort and free interest than of compulsion and forced application, and the natural means of study in youth is play.[3]

The Creative Dramatics Movement pioneered by the American Winifred Ward, the Theatre-in-Education Movement, which is of British origin, and such advocates of Theatre in Education as Peter Slade, Brian Way, Dorothy Heathcote, Nellie McCaslin, and Richard Courtney, have clearly demonstrated that theatre is, indeed, an important and effective educational tool.

Any over-emphasis of the entertainment characteristic is, therefore, unfortunate because it overshadows the ideological essence of the theatre. It is even more regrettable in Africa, where traditional societies provide very striking examples of the ideological role of theatre. Theatre was a tool for instruction and transmission

---

1. Ibid.
2. Dewey, John 1968, as quoted in Courtney, R., *Play, Drama and Thought*, Drama Book Specialists, New York.
3. Cook, C. 1917, *The Play Way*, Heinemann, London.

of knowledge, values and attitudes in initiation rites, marriage, death, religious rituals or public forums for behavioural appraisal, criticism and control. Dance, drama, mime, story-telling, and heroic recitations were an essential part of one's upbringing. In his study on Ghanaian traditional theatre Scott observes that it

> evokes the wisdom and authority of the ancestors ... it speaks of a way of life one ought to live. It outlines the social responsibilities and speaks of family loyalties. Frequently, masks and symbols, which serve literally as teaching aids, are used. Often they are considered principle instruments of social control. They speak clearly and sharply with respect to the role, the relationship and the responsibility of an African people.[1]

Similarly Traore's study on West Africa theatre observes that "the theatre takes its place in a framework of institutions whose aim is to make the members of a society accept certain common values ... thus it contributes to the control and the integration of feelings and beliefs".[2] Fiebach also argues that the social function of the traditional African theatre was of first importance: "It played a decisive role in instructing the youth, in familiarising them with values and socially-required attitudes. It was the medium in which the history and religion of various tribes and clans were handed down to successive generations."[3] Citing the example of South African story-telling Leshoai says, that "On a moonlit night the children sit at the feet of their grandmothers to be educated and entertained in intimate theatre for the young people".[4] And the Swedish-Tanzanian cultural co-operation Karibu Project report has the following to say about Tanzanian traditional theatre:

> Music is used along with dance to preserve, and to teach laws, history, religion, how to take care of your health etc. Song, music and dance take the place of our (Swedish) books in some parts of traditional African education. With most folk groups this education takes place in pre-puberty, before young people are accepted into the circle of adults by the cere-

---

1. Kennedy, Scott 1973, *In Search of African Theatre*, Charles Scribner's Sons, New York.
2. Traore, B. 1972, *The Black African Theatre and its Social Function*, (trans. D. Adelugba), Ibadan University Press, Ibadan.
3. Fiebach, J. 1972, "The Social Function of Modern African Theatre and Brecht", *Darlite*, University of Dar es Salaam, Vol. 4, No. 2.
4. Leshoai, B. 1975, *Drama as a Means of Education in Africa*, Ph.D. thesis, University of Dar es Salaam.

mony which is usually called the rite of initiation ... These studies are ordinarily carried on in secret societies in which music and dance play a large role as carriers of knowledge.[1]

The present author also deals in detail with the educational role of African Theatre in her study *Tanzanian Traditional Theatre as a Pedagogical Institution*.[2]

In a way it is surprising how contemporary African political regimes manage to ignore this more significant function of theatre while at the same time they opt for the promotion and assertion of national cultural identities. For example, despite the distinct educational function of traditional African theatre, today theatre is separated from education and rarely forms part of the formal educational system. Contemporary educators do not often consider theatre as relevant for education and often resist any attempt to introduce theatre into the schools.[3] It is ironic that formal education systems in Africa, mostly copied from the Western world, continue to exclude theatre from educational methodology despite the fact that in these very Western education systems, theatre is increasingly being emphasised. This is especially true in Britain, the country which most often serves as the African model. Theatre which does take place in the schools is generally in the form of play productions and rarely African dance. It is often only an extra curricular activity, a pastime. Theatre may communicate educational messages but is rarely looked upon as education. Tanzania is perhaps the only country in Africa where theatre is a teaching subject in some schools, and where the presence of theatre performances in the schools is by deliberate ideological design.

Emphasis on the entertainment function of theatre in Africa today is, as mentioned before, a deliberate and convenient move to suppress the potential of theatre as a tool for raising the consciousness of the people. It is difficult to imagine that all the per-

---

1. Karibu project—Ngoma, Music and Dance in Tanzania, 1974, mimeo, Ministry of Youth and Culture, Dar es Salaam.
2. Mlama, P. 1983, *Tanzanian Traditional Theatre as a Pedagogical Institution*, Ph.D. thesis, University of Dar es Salaam.
3. See Debebe, E. et al. 1986, *Report on the Mission to Evaluate the Training of Performing Artists in Ethiopia and Tanzania for ACTPA*, mimeo, Union of African Performing Artists, Yaounde.

sonnel in the ministries of culture and other government institutions responsible for theatre promotion are unaware of the fact that there is more to African dance than performing at airports and state banquets or singing unlimited praises to the political leaders.

The neo-colonial character of many African countries explains their tendency to perpetuate the entertainment-based theatre imposed on them by their colonial masters. Many theatre practitioners are busy with European theatre audiences in Africa and abroad. Successful productions in New York or London become the measure of achievement of African theatre directors even if no rapport is established with the local audiences. The number of irrelevant and unadapted productions of foreign plays on African stages is still embarrassingly high.

The perpetuation of the "art for art's sake" function of theatre, however, is not restricted to the staging of foreign plays. For over twenty years the movement for African theatre has been in force. Many theatre groups have emerged and propagated Africanness in the form and content of theatre in Africa. Numerous African plays have appeared to bear witness as the fruits of this movement. African playwrights of international fame (Soyinka, Clark, J de Graft, Ruganda, Ngugi, Hussein) are products of this movement. Plays relevant to African realities are no longer a problem. Numerous dance troupes have also been formed to capture the rich African cultural traditions. The Nigerian Folk Opera, the Concert Party in Ghana and Togo, and the Koteba in Mali have all established themselves as permanent theatre institutions.

However, although these theatre efforts emerged out of the African theatrical heritage, many of them have not succeeded in perpetuating and transferring to the present the ideological functions of African indigenous theatre. Instead, the capitalist conditions under which the contemporary theatre companies operate force them to commoditise their artistic talents and succumb to the box-office by emphasising entertainment. The theatre directors often leave good plays for more frivolous choices in order to survive financially. Similarly those dealing with traditional dances have discarded most of the educational characteristics and remain with only that which entertains. The owner of the Super Fanaka Dance Troupe in Dar es Salaam states that his group's aim is "to entertain the customers who visit his bar".[1] The managing director of DDC Kibisa confirmed that the troupe is a commercial enterprise. The preservation and development of Tanzanian culture, as one of the objectives, is secondary to money-making through providing entertainment for the public.[2]

Waist and hip dance movements are preferred to other movements because of the titillation effects and thus the greater capacity for attracting large audiences. This explains, for instance, why the hip swaying *Sindimba* Makonde dance, originally an initiation into adulthood dance, took the Tanzanian entertainment circles by storm and has remained in the repertory of all commercial dance troupes since 1970.

All this, unfortunately, is an indication of the effects of increased penetration of capitalist culture and the consequent breakdown of traditional cultural structures where theatre was not merely entertainment.

Theatre in socialist-oriented countries like Guinea, Mozambique, and Tanzania has attempted to exploit the potential of theatre for consciousness-raising. Much success has been achieved in mobilising the people to support socialist ideologies, but as mentioned earlier, theatre here has been turned into vehicles of blunt political propaganda. One gets too many dance songs that blindly repeat what the ruling Parties or government leaders say, sometimes even generating meaningless songs like the following:

Chama Chama Chama	Party Party Party
Cha Mapinduzi Tanzania	Revolutionary (Party) in Tanzania
Ee Chama Tanzania	Yes the Party in Tanzania[3]

Tanzania's Mathias Mnyampala's poetic dramas, *Ngonjera*, such as "Azimio la Arusha", "Elimu ya Kujitegemea"[4], are good examples

---

1. Mbwana, A. 1984, *The Contribution of Modern Dance Troupes towards the Development of Traditional African Theatre*, Independent study, mimeo, Department of Art, Music and Theatre, University of Dar es Salaam.
2. Songoyi, M. 1983, *Commercialisation, its Impact on Traditional Dances*, Department of Art, Music and Theatre, mimeo, University of Dar es Salaam.
3. *Ibid.*
4. Mnyampala, M. 1970, *Ngonjera za Ukuta*, East African Literature Bureau, Dar es Salaam.

of the faithful paraphrasing of Party policies without any artistic interpretation.

The use of theatre for the maintenance of the status quo is, however, not unique to socialist-oriented countries. Many regimes in Africa have found theatre, especially traditional dance, a convenient tool for trumpeting praises, often undeserved, for the leaders and ruling parties in order to make people forget that they have failed to produce the goods for their constituents. As mentioned earlier, traditional dances have become an indispensable adornment of government and party public appearances.

The above is a misuse of the ideological potential of theatre to benefit a few, namely, the ruling class. In fact even the entertainment theatre in the cities is for the consumption of the urban few with the ability to buy their entertainment. For the majority, especially in the rural areas, the value of their theatre still lies in its ideological functions. That is why people still participate in initiation of wedding dances without charging or paying for it. The content of such performances displays the use of theatre to instruct, criticise, ridicule, praise and generally to shape a people's consciousness to societal beliefs.[1]

This theatre is still very much alive, contrary to a belief among the urban elite who, because of their own uprooting from the rural areas, thinks that all life in Africa has been modernised and all cultural expressions replaced by radio, books or television. The elite theatre artists, in their attempt to take theatre to the people through the travelling theatre and theatre for development, discussed in Chapter 4, have found that the people's popular theatre forms are still active. Because theatre is so much a part of people's lives, even the colonial onslaught on culture through education or Christianity did not manage to eliminate these theatre forms. They have, in most cases, only been modified in response to the socio-economic changes. The big problem is that they have been ignored by the urban-based ruling classes. In the absence of modern communication these forms have continued to provide about the only communication forum through which the rural areas are exchanging ideas and expressing their views about life. Media studies have confirmed that, in spite of all that has been done to develop

---

1. Leshoai, *op. cit.*

the technological media—radio, film, television, and print—the majority of the rural population in Africa still has no access to it.[1]

The rural populations have, therefore, continued to use their own communication media, including the theatre. The UNESCO campaign in the 1970s for the use of folk media for development communication in the Third World was based on the realisation of the existence of such media. As such, there are still many people in Africa accustomed and exposed to a theatre whose value lies in its ability to express the people's feelings, concerns and aspirations and to portray values and attitudes necessary to the continued well-being of the society.

It is for this reason that theatre carries the potential to become a tool for cultivating and promoting the culture of a people. As an ideological tool, it has the ability to promote and inculcate cultural values of any system. It has, throughout history, been used as an ideological tool for the dominant classes.

In the Philippines for example, Tiongson observes that

> through the *Komedya* theatre form, the Spaniards had succeeded in creating and propagating among the natives a colonial mentality that made them look up to the Spaniards as the more beautiful specimen of humanity, as the species favoured by the gods and as the superior race they must imitate and idolise ... For as the native looked at the image of Christ in the *Sinakulo*, he saw a Christ whose main virtue was the ability to shed tears and to compete acceptance of all the suffering dealt him by his oppressors. To be Christ-like then was to accept all the suffering in this life—mainly those dealt by friars and the Spaniards.[2]

The old Peking opera of China, the Kabuki and Noh of Japan, Sanskrit drama of India, the mainstream theatre of Europe and America, including West End and Broadway, are but a few examples of theatres which are in the service of the ideology of the dominant classes. But the dominated classes have also used theatre to enhance an ideology vital to the struggles against their oppressors. Such has been the case in many parts of the world where production relations have produced classes of exploited people whose conditions of life inevitably gave rise to struggles for change and liberation. The struggles of the exploited masses have

---

1. Worldview Information Foundation, *op. cit.*
2. Thiongson, N. ed. 1984, *The Politics of Culture: The Philippines Experience*, PETA, Manila.

taken many forms varying from hostility and resistance to outright armed struggles or revolutions. For example, refusal to offer vital labour, or sabotage activities such as destroying crops or agricultural machinery, have been common forms of peasant resistance to the feudal systems of Asia. Kennedy cites an example of the landless peasants of a Malaysian rice farming village in Kedah state refusing to plant rice for landlords, who then hired a combine harvester thus depriving the peasants of their much needed wages from rice harvesting.[1]

Workers' strikes are common in all capitalist modes of industrial production and serve as another example of resistance by the exploited. Such resistances reveal anger, indignation or opposition to what they regard as unjust or unfair actions by others more wealthy or powerful than they. Through such resistance people struggle to affirm what they regard as just or unjust treatment and conditions.

Resistance has often developed into organised popular movements, political and/or military, through which the exploited have fought to overthrow the dominant powers and to bring about transformation. The revolutions in Cuba, China, France, and Nicaragua are but a few examples.

These struggles for liberation, whether in the form of isolated economic sabotage or organised political or military action, have in most cases also involved the use of popular arts. Popular songs, poetry, dance, and drama have been employed by the struggling masses to vent their anger or to inspire the struggles and boost the morale of the participants as well as to conscientise them for the right causes.

The employment of popular arts for the struggle of the exploited classes has taken a variety of forms. There are those spontaneous and unorganised artistic creations of individual artists who are inspired to create poems or songs that decry the suffering of the masses as the following examples from China and India illustrate:[2]

---

1. Kennedy, S. 1973.
2. Curwen, C. 1974, "Two Folk Songs from China", *The Journal of Peasant Studies*, Frank Cass and Co., Vol. 1, No. 4, July.

In the winter cold without clothes
it's hard to survive.
The master is very unjust:
When it rains he docks my pay,
When it's fine he curses me for
knocking off too early.

When you use a man's bowl he's
got control,
When you eat a man's food it
means servitude.
At the Fifth Watch before dawn
I have to be out;
But I only get home when the
heaven is full of stars.

If there's anger it is mine,
If there's sorrow it is mine,
In the evening I take a cup to
borrow some oil.

We poor—
The sun scorches us, the rain soaks us.
Never mind the sun, never mind the rain—
All you get in the end is a pocketful
of debts.

What bitter misery!
On New Year's Eve there's only gruel to eat.
The children see that others have cakes
And come home crying to ask their mother why.

When others walk down the road I step aside
And never walk down the middle.
If I think to open my mouth and say something,
They say a poor man's words are not worth
hearing.

The Rashtriya Seva Dal song from India express the suffering in the following way:[1]

> Chorus: Come, come you poor, come, take
>   the flag in hand
>   Listen to the toilers' cry!
>   Moneylenders' rule cannot be endured,
>   Now it must be destroyed!
>
> Inside the purple cars see the painted dolls
> Comfortably they go on the road—
> Thorns in the jungle, his bare feet are mangled,
> The poor man walks with his load.
>
> Story upon story, decorations gaudy,
> Their houses are blinding our eyes—
> Huts made of mud, darkness inside,
> Heavy the poor man's fate lies.
>
> Plates made of silver, designs surrounding,
> Sweets to eat their fill—
> Pots made of clay, the food is decayed,
> The poor have no holiday meal.
>
> Now comes the summer, curtains are scented
> To keep the hot breeze at bay—
> For the poor only a tree's umbrella
> And a dog for company today.
>
> The hookah needs lighting, a servant is waiting,
> There is wood for the winter around—
> The poor man has hardly a rag for his body,
> And sleeps on the stony ground!
>
> The flag of revolution, the call to insurrection,
> Listen to the toilers' cry!
> For ending injustice, destroying oppression
> The moment of truth is nigh—

---

1. Omvedt, Gail 1977, "Revolutionary Music from India", *The Journal of Peasant Studies*, Frank Cass and Co., Vol. 4, No. 3, April.

Come, come you poor, come, take the flag in hand,
Listen to the toilers' cry,
Moneylenders' rule cannot be endured,
Now it must be destroyed!

There are many examples of playwrights, poets or musicians who have gone to jail or been exiled for speaking out for the masses. Biswas cites the example of Mukanda Das in Bengali who was sent to jail for his Swadeshi Jatra plays which were directed against British colonialism.[1]

The employment of the popular arts sometimes takes the form of cultural or social movements through which specific political causes are pushed forward. In 19th century Mediterranean France, for example, popular artistic expressions were employed by the peasantry to effectively mobilise support for political changes. Rural radicalism was intertwined with popular culture and there was an integration of new political ideas into the rhythm of religious and secular communal festivals with their vibrant patterns of processions, songs and dances.[2]

The carnivals of Europe or the Caribbean Islands, though often considered mere cultural festivals, have been significant political movements through which the lower ranks have expressed their views about their conditions. Through the process of "reversal" they have ridiculed and attacked the status quo. As McPhee observes, the essence of the carnival lies in its parody of the constraints of the real world. By investing and mocking reality, he argues, the carnival presents a new world. "To a world of sickness, poverty and hunger is opposed one of indulgence and excess. To social hierarchy, laws imposed by outsiders and intrusive police, carnival poses egalitarianism, communal autonomy and popular justice. Through masquerades, sexual taboos are transgressed and sex roles reversed. Carnival culminates on the judgement of the carnival symbol, the mannequin or dummy and its punishment by storming, burning, beating or beheading."[3]

---

1. Biswas, K. 1983, *Political Theatre in Bengal*, mimeo, The India People's Theatre Association (IPTA).
2. McPhee, P. 1978, "Popular Culture, Symbolism and Rural Radicalism in Nineteenth Century France", *Journal of Peasant Studies*, Vol. 5, No. 2, January.
3. *Ibid*.

Jean-Pierre Gravel gives an account of how in the 1960s, theatre in Quebec played an important role in the "Quebec for the Quebecoise" movement that sought to disengage Quebec from Anglo/Canadian domination. He cites Le Theatre Euh as one politically active group in that movement. Despite a police order forbidding the company to stage performances in the street, Le Theatre Euh persevered, taking their performances to audiences of workers they wanted to reach with their message. Le Theatre Euh would come to a mining town where a strike was in progress or threatened and with their short theatrical presentations, articulate the miners' anger at the aloofness of multinational companies who seemed to own their lives along with all the real estate of the town. Le Theatre Euh also supported the farmers' protest of the construction of the Mirabel airport. The site for the new airstrip was situated about 25 miles from Montreal and required expropriation of hundreds of acres of arable land. A play was developed to explain the farmers' position, as recorded from the families who housed the actors during the several weeks of research and production. The actors based their style on the Comedia dell'Arte which gave a constant background to texts which changed according to the issue under examination. The audience would be encouraged to provide rhythmic accompaniment by playing on spoons, a sound which has reverberated through generations of music-making in Quebec.[1]

The 1960s and 1970s saw a strong Black American Theatre movement that was a response to the civil rights and Black consciousness movements. The Black Americans saw in theatre a weapon through which they could assert the dignity of their race and voice their demands against discrimination. Rejecting mainstream theatre, which served the elite white people's interests, they created their Black theatre movement with a form and content that could push forward the cause of Black Americans. Speaking for the "Minority Theatre", one of the many artistic movements at the time, George Baas argues that theatre, to the minority Americans, is not something merely to be enjoyed but something that makes the folk uncomfortable with their lot and determined

---

1. Gravel, J. 1983, "Popular Theatre in Quebec", *Theaterwork Magazine*, House of Print, Minnesota, Vol. 3, No. 5, July/August.

to change it. It must challenge the status quo, come to grips with the real American world, attack the problems confronted by real people, and give insights into those problems:

> Minority peoples deserve a theatre that sharpens our understanding of the workings of our pluralistic society. Minority plays, if they are to contribute to the quality of life, they must not pretend that serious social problems do not exist.[1]

The Yannge theatre movement in China was, in the 1940s, one of the forces through which the Chinese Communist Party raised the consciousness of the rural masses to support the revolution. The CCP believed that art was a reflection of the economic base of a society. As such any revolution to change the economic base had to include the employment of art to reflect the revolution and to promote transformation. At the 1942 Talks at the Yenan Forum on Literature and Art, Mao unambiguously stressed the vital role of culture in the revolution by stating that:

> ... for the liberation of the Chinese nation there are various fronts, among which there are the front of the pen and of the gun, the cultural and the military fronts. To defeat the enemy we must rely primarily on the army with guns. But this army alone is not enough; we must also have a cultural army, which is absolutely indispensable for writing for our own ranks and defeating the enemy.[2]

The Yannge theatre movement was one way of integrating the cultural front into the revolution. Yannge was a traditional peasant theatrical form consisting of dance, instrumental and vocal music, and dialogue. Its form relied on simple humorous and farcical content, type characters, minimal theatrical properties and outdoor staging. Such a form rendered it suitable for accommodating new messages. Its accessibility to the peasantry made it a more effective mobilising force than the more intellectual dramas written by the elite artists.

All these examples go to show that there has always been a close relationship between theatre and the welfare of a society. As an ideological tool it has the potential to effect change and to contribute towards bettering living conditions. The oppressed classes,

---

1. Baas, G. 1976, *Minority Theatre*, mimeo, Brown University.
2. Mao Tse-tung, *op. cit.*

in their struggles against oppression, have channelled this potential into Popular Theatre—the primary concern of this study.

CHAPTER 3
Popular theatre in Latin America and Asia

It is important to recognise the fact that Popular Theatre is a movement not confined to Africa. The twentieth century has seen a significant evolution of Popular Theatre in various parts of the developing world where struggles against political, economic, and cultural domination have been the order of the day. The long history of anti-feudal, anti-colonial and anti-imperialist struggles has now been meshed with peasant struggles against national dominant classes who, with the assistance of foreign capital, seek to consolidate their economic, social, and political power. The increasing penetration of multinational capital into the developing countries, growing class divisions, landlessness, unemployment and abject poverty, have pushed the peasants and workers into struggles for structural changes.

The oppressed groups have recognised the potential of Popular Theatre as an effective weapon in the struggles for land, better working and living conditions, and other basic rights. In Asia and Latin America, like in Africa, Popular Theatre forms were used for national liberation movements.[1] But even after independence from colonialism, the people have continued to use this theatre to confront the forces that continue to subject them to poverty and misery.

In this chapter we will review several Latin American and Asian examples of the use of theatre for such purposes.

The Philippines offer one example. In spite of liberation from both Spanish and American colonisation, the Filipino have been continuously subjected to some of the worst forms of exploitation culminating in the 1972 martial law by the Marcos regime. The

---

1. See Kidd, R. and M. Rashid 1984, "Theatre by the People, for the People and of the People: People's Theatre and Landless Organisation in Bangladesh", *Bulletin of Concerned Asian Scholars*, Vol. 16, No. 1.

plight of the peasant is well articulated in the following statement by the *Kilusang Magbukid ng Pilipinas*, a peasant organisation:

> We, the Filipino peasantry, create and produce the food and other basic needs of society. We work the land to bring forth bountiful harvests. Yet we often go hungry. For many years we have tilled the land paid for in blood and bequeathed to us by our forefathers. This is a legacy we have cherished and for which we have offered so much sacrifice. Yet our right to own land, to be free from feudal bondage has always been denied us ... We comprise the majority of the toiling masses. Yet we suffer the worst forms of feudal oppression from foreign capitalists, big landlords, bureaucrats and compradors. They refuse to give us our just rewards. They do not give us meaningful participation in determining the destiny of our nation.[1]

The Philippine economy is semi-feudal and semi-colonial in character. Foreign capital dominates the country's strategic sectors including agriculture where transnational companies and big landlords own most of the land and control agricultural trade. The unrestricted entry of foreign capital has resulted in the serious depletion of natural resources, increased monopoly of land-holding, decreased food production for home consumption, and it has uprooted and impoverished thousands of poor peasants. An escalating militarisation and US support for the regime have considerably curtailed human rights and civil liberties and pushed a large portion of the population into a life of misery.

Horfilla observes, however, that "in spite of the attempts to make the people passive, submissive and cowed through harassment, imprisonment and even murder, the people are slowly on the rise. There is massive conscientisation and organisation evolving in the countryside, in factories, in the universities, in the communities and other settings".[2] The situation has led to an urgent need for a cultural movement to support the struggle through depicting the people's plight and expressing their felt needs and, more significantly, to conscientise them into a better understanding of their situation and a creative participation in the struggle.

---

1. Kilusang Magbukiding Pilipinas 1986, *Policy Proposals on Agriculture and Countryside Development*, Quezon city.
2. Horfilla, N. 1984, "Theatre in Mindanao" in Tiongson ed., *The Politics of Culture. The Philippines Experience*, PETA, Manila.

In his article, "The History of the Growth and Development of Creative Dramatics in Mindanao-Sulu Philippines" Carl Gaspar outlines the development of a community theatre movement geared towards conscientisation of the poor, deprived, and oppressed, so as to enable them to organise against their oppressive forces. The community theatre movement, run under the auspices of the Catholic church, which unlike many churches elsewhere, often has taken the side of the oppressed, is an attempt to provide the masses with an alternative medium through which they can articulate their position. It is rooted in the community and incorporates the realities of life as felt by the members of the community. People's maximum participation is the core of the process with outsiders acting only as facilitators, stimulators and change agents. Local people are also trained in the skills of running community theatre so that the community can run its own conscientisation programmes on a long term basis.

A more important characteristic of the Philippine community theatre movement is its effort to make theatre also an agent for community organisation. "The whole concept of community theatre is not complete if there is no corresponding conscious effort at organising the people around issues that affect their lives, thereby developing communal action tailored to their needs," Gaspar says.[1] The Philippine Educational Theatre Association (PETA) has been quite instrumental in training community theatre artists both in theatrical and organisational skills. And even though this has not yet resulted in the total liberation of the people, it has produced some radical stirrings and some awareness amongst its participants. Carl Gaspar remarked a few months before he was imprisoned in 1984, that:

> The movement has provided promise for the years to come. Within the current perspective, it has already been integrated into the historical phase of a people's struggle towards their national aspirations, and will stay as the forum through which the Filipino soul can communicate, in search for a more liberating view.[2]

---

1. Gaspar, K. "The History of the Growth and Development of Creative Dramatics in Mindanao-Sulu, Philippines", *International Popular Theatre Alliance Newsletter*, Vol. 3.
2. *Ibid.*

Nicaragua is an outstanding example of the integration of a popular movement into a revolutionary struggle. The repression and atrocities of the Anastasio Somoza regime (1973–1979) necessitated the formation of mass movements that sought to liberate the Nicaraguan people. Apart from the Sandinista military movement whose armed struggle eventually deposed Somoza, there were several other movements that served as the base for organising at the grassroot level. Associacion de Trabajadores del Campo (ATC, The Farmworkers Union) was such a movement. Under this organisation the farmworkers fought very fiercely for their land and facilitated the effective participation of the rural population in the revolution.

The ATC saw the importance of the cultural work from the beginning of the struggle. As Nidia Bustos, one of its members, said:

> It is not only with arms that a revolution is made. Revolution is made in every moment of one's life and our experience confirms this. It is made with music because the guitar, too, was aimed and was fired to the point where the guitar and the gun got mixed up. Revolution is also made by writing poetry and by organising popular education.[1]

ATC used the campesinos' own cultural expressions as tools for horizontal communication, conscientisation and organisation for the armed struggle against the Somoza dictatorship. So, like other movements, including the Sandinista Youth Movement, ATC organised its own cultural arm with people who moved among farmworkers, assisting, motivating and encouraging cultural performances for the struggle. With the revolutionary struggle grew a dynamic people's culture.

> It is not as if the culture of the people did not exist. But it is as if it had died and had to be reborn, to be reincarnated in the revolution, in the struggle of the people. That is why we call it popular culture, because it is the fruit of the daily tasks, the struggles and the suffering of the people.[2]

The Los Alpes, Frente Sur, and Cadil de Pueblo theatre groups were born out of this popular culture. They developed performances of short skits, songs, dances and poetry and put these on for their own community. The hard life of the people, filled with

---

1. Bustos 1982.
2. *Ibid.*

repression, frequent tortures and murder was portrayed in these performances. What was emphasised, however, was the portrayal of a positive way forward, the need for the people to take action to rout the oppressive forces. The performances often developed into open discussions with everyone present, during which issues were clarified and strategies for action charred out. This theatre work had to be conducted under cover and was constantly under the threat of repression. In 1978 the Los Alpes group had to burn all their property and masks, because Somoza's Guardia Nacional was coming to arrest the members. The group had to disband and most of its members left the village to join the guerrillas in the mountains.

In the years after the revolution, more than eighty theatre groups emerged in Nicaragua to carry on the revolution, both in the wake of the counter-revolution by the *contras* and to facilitate national reconstruction. In Nicaragua it is taken for granted that art, particularly popular music and theatre, is in the service of the construction of the new society. It serves as a means of communication between regions, a forum for discussing the reconstruction programmes, and a vehicle for political consciousness-raising.[1]

The Sandinista government formed the Movement of Peasant Artistic and Theatrical Expression, MECATE (Movimento de Expresion Campesino Artistica) to co-ordinate the people's popular artistic activity for the continuing revolution. MECATE functioned as the cultural arm of the farmworkers' movement with responsibility to organise various cultural activities among which are the *veladas*, similar to the Zimbabwean *Pungwe* to be mentioned in chapter 4. A *velada* is an evening of entertainment, news-sharing, discussion and socialising at the community level. During a *velada*, local groups put on short improvised skits, and everyone joins in the songs and dances at the end of each *velada*. Community discussion, education, and even fund-raising are included in a *velada* evening. MECATE also organised inter-group cultural exchange, campaigns to raise morale, and the understanding of national reconstruction issues.

Bustos, the co-ordinator of MECATE, describes the popular theatre process in Nicaragua as follows:

---

1. See Brookes, C., *International Popular Theatre Alliance Newsletter*, Toronto.

> The group members bring the problems they face each day in their lives, in the workplace, the community, their work in the militia or their family life. Sometimes they might be approached by other villages, other organisations or even the administrator of a state farm to deal with a certain problem or topic. If the topic is sufficiently interesting they might take it up as a theme and develop it into a play ... Once the group decides on a problem, they go out and do some research, finding out what the people are saying about the problem. This research also attempts to discover the expressions and images that the people use in talking about the problems and these are incorporated into the play ... Group meetings and rehearsals are open and other community members often drop in. The plot is developed collectively and everyone joins in suggesting changes as the play is developed.[1]

ISAS, (Centro de Informacion y Servicio de Asesoria en Salud), is an organisation which specialised in the promotion of the use of theatre for popular health education. Health workers and medical personnel, including the University of Managua medical students, were trained in the use of puppetry, storytelling, and other popular theatre forms as a methodology for working with the village population.[2]

Popular Theatre has also gained importance in other Latin American countries, which are characterised by repression from dictatorial regimes, as well as economic and cultural domination from imperialist forces. The importance of Popular Theatre was emphasised in the Latin American Conference on Popular Theatre held in Ecuador in 1977, which brought together thirty-two groups from eleven Latin American countries. This conference produced a statement pledging its continued commitment to Popular Theatre. They expressed this as a search for the equality of classes within the Latin American society, in which art is relegated to a secondary position and the people to non-participation. Popular Theatre was seen as an indispensable form of struggle for the transformation of Latin American society, to rescue the rich artistic heritage of the people and to integrate the popular creative potential into the movement for a popular, independent and eman-

---

1. Bustos 1982.
2. Interview with Maria Zuniga, Co-ordinator of ISAS, May 1988, Uppsala.

cipating art.[1] Carlos and Graciela Nunez also gave an account of Popular Theatre in community organisation in Mexico.[2]

The sub-contintent of India, which also has witnessed brutal forms of exploitation and oppression—not only through feudalism, colonisation, and imperialism, but also through the Brahmanic caste system that bonds its lower castes to a life worse than slavery—has of necessity produced remarkable examples of the use of Popular Theatre in the struggle of the masses against economic, social and cultural bondage.

Kalpena Biswas outlines a long history of Popular Theatre in Bengal.[3] He describes the thirteenth century folk art form called *Bhakti*, which was based on song and dance, and which attacked the Brahmanic system and called for a more egalitarian order. British colonial rule also provoked various forms of resistance theatre, one of which was the Swadeshi Jatra of Mukunda Das travelling troupe mentioned earlier in Chapter 2. Mukunda Das adapted Jatra, a traditional form dealing with mythological and historical themes, to decry colonial injustices, feudal exploitation, and caste oppression.

At the height of the nationalist struggle against British rule in the 1940s, the various resistance theatre movements resulted in the formation of the Indian People's Theatre Association (IPTA). IPTA mobilised songs, dances, puppetry, and other popular art forms to expose such colonial injustices as the 1943 British-induced Bengal famine that claimed the lives of five million peasants. IPTA was closely linked to leftist political movements, especially the Communist Party of India. Together with the Youth Cultural Institute (YCI) and the Anti-Fascist Writers' and Artists' Association (AFWAA), IPTA sought to convince the masses that they were the masters of their own destiny and the repository of the forces of change. Using folk forms, such as *Tamasha* and *Burrakattha*, IPTA attempted to mould people's own popular forms to function as a weapon with which to fight their enemies. Themes

---

1. Bustos 1982.
2. See Nunez, Garcia and Carlos 1980, "Popular Theatre, Popular Education and Urban Community Organisation in Mexico" in Kidd, R. and N. Colleta eds., *Tradition for Development*, German Foundation for International Development, Berlin.
3. See Kidd, R. and N. Colleta eds.

for performances included colonial and feudal exploitation, the oppression of women, autocracy and cruelty to workers in the mills.

Even though IPTA disintegrated with the political developments after India's independence in 1947 which saw the partition of the sub-continent into India and Pakistan as well as the repression of the Communist movement by the national bourgeoisie, the seeds of Popular Theatre continued to sprout. Among the Harijans (outcaste) Popular Theatre has become one of the most effective tools of fighting the feudal lords under whom they continue to slave. In India the outcaste, who are at the lowest rung of the caste ladder, have suffered the most from the underdevelopment caused by India's development policy. India's policy of mass industrialisation and the "Green Revolution" had the consequence of throwing the country deeper into the claws of international capital and accentuating the entrenchment of capitalism. It has been said of the "Green Revolution" that although

> the new seeds, fertilizer, mechanisation and the capitalist farming methods did raise productivity it also polarised the class structure, fattening and capitalising the rich farmers, reducing the proportion of middle farmers, forcing the smaller farmers into debt and producing massive landlessness, unemployment and impoverishment. The rich farmers ... maintained their domination over and exploitation of the poor farmers and landless labourers.[1]

The Harijans came off the worst, and this resulted in the formation of the Action for Cultural and Political Change (ACPC) movement that sought to politicise and organise the Harijans to fight for their basic rights and better working and living conditions. Kidd gives a detailed account of how the movement, initiated in 1974, operates.[2] Motivated by outrage at the daily humiliation, and disillusioned by the impotence of conventional development strategies a group of Harijan university graduates embarked on the establishment of the ACPC in the Tamil Nadu region.

Kidd describes the ACPC approach as involving a community-based animateur and a long process of organisation and conscientisation of the Harijans to take action against their exploitation.

---

1. *Ibid.*
2. *Ibid.*

The animateur lives in a village and gets to know the people and their problems to win their confidence. After about a month, the animateur calls a mass meeting and explains the objectives of the ACPC whose goal is to build up a labourers' movement through which the people themselves will confront the landlords and other oppressive powers. During these discussions, theatre in the form of improvised skits, role playing, music, song and mime, is used as a process of analysis and building confidence in the people. Between each skit, the actors discuss the problems with the audience, challenging them to do something about the problems. Then the drama shows people coming together and taking action on issues such as water, house sites or electricity through petitioning the authorities concerned. The show identifies the enemy, caricatures the key powerful figures and exposes their corrupt or exploitative practices. Strategies for organising the labourers such as strikes, mass rallies, hunger strikes and the possible reactions of the landlord and other oppressors are portrayed. An important aspect of the drama is the inclusion of an analysis of the historical economic and social formations to make the people understand the workings of the feudal or capitalist system. This gives the participants a more critical view of their situation and a better understanding of the action they have to take to make their struggle worthwhile.

Kidd describes one popular theatre experience he witnessed as follows:

> The programme begins at 7 pm with revolutionary songs to attract the labourers returning from the fields. The whole village gathers around the stage area. The actors are some of the villagers and a few animateurs. The play is unscripted. The actors have agreed on a scenario beforehand and each one improvises his or her lines. They caricature their oppressors with real insight into their idiosyncrasies. The play is a number of skits on various problems linked through the principal character, who acts as a narrator (commentator, landlord, landlord's servant, youth leader) who appears throughout the play. Songs are performed between each skit.
>
> The play opens with a song by the clown about the Harijan girl who puts on saris and jewelry like a caste girl but still is ostracised, and another one caricaturing a Harijan traditional leader who boasts about his importance yet is shown to be simply the landlord's stooge. The rest of the drama shows a bonded labourer remaining loyal to his landlord and being tricked into signing a false bond paper, the landlord in collusion with the government officials attempting to appropriate drought relief

funds meant for a Harijan village, a trader adulterating his goods, and money-lending at exhobitant rates, Harijan initiatives being undermined by religion, alcohol and manipulations by the landlord.[1]

The performance is followed by a planning meeting where everybody participates to strategise on the follow-up action. If the suggested action is a strike, the audience discusses how to effectively organise the strike: overcoming gears, choosing the most strategic time such as during harvest, stopping labourers from other villages coming to diffuse the strike, surviving without wages during the strike, informing the police so as to avoid misrepresentations from the landlords, terms and conditions for the strike and the anticipated retaliation from the landlords.

The ACPC has scored considerable success in effectively organising the Harijans through this process. In Chitammoor area in Chinglepet district, between 1974 and 1977, ACPC work resulted in the formation of a strong agricultural labourers' movement which took over their own organising from ACPC and by 1978 had won two major wage strikes, obtained written agreements from the landlord to stop all beatings, taken possession of farming land and sites, released a number of families from bonded labour and successfully petitioned local authorities for many basic services.[2]

The socio-economic situation in Bangladesh, which is not very different from that of India in its feudal, capitalist and caste character has also made the use of Popular Theatre for organising the landless peasants a necessity. The peasant and worker of Bangladesh had hoped that the war of liberation from Pakistan and the independence in 1971 would bring about a true revolution, the smashing of the feudal system and land reform that would distribute land to everybody. Soon, however, it was clear that not only were the fruits of independence monopolised by the ruling class but also the feudal structures remained the same and the penetration of capitalist and imperialist forces intensified leaving more than half the population landless and unemployed.

The political turmoil, expressed in the frequent violent clashes between the power of the state and the masses or the students is

---

1. Kidd, R. and M. Rashid.
2. *Ibid.*

an inevitable result of the widening gap between the rich and the poor. This dissatisfaction with the situation has led to the formation of various movements that seek solutions to the suffering of the common people. Proshika is one such movement. It is a rural animation organisation with animateurs who are permanently based in the villages to work with landless labourers in a process of popular education and organisation. In each village the Proshika animateurs form groups of fifteen to twenty landless labourers who meet regularly, build up trust in each other, eliminate conflicts among themselves, overcome dependence on the money-lender through collective savings, talk about their problems of exploitation and victimisation and along with other groups organise struggles to confront injustice and corruption by the landlords and to demand better working conditions.

Like ACPC in India, Proshika found the use of Popular Theatre in consciousness raising, problem analysis and confidence building quite effective in organising the landless peasants. Theatre was, therefore, incorporated into the training workshops of the leaders of the landless peasants. The peasants immediately applied the theatrical approach by organising their own theatre groups through which they portrayed their real life experiences of losing land, going into debt, exploitation, beatings by the landlords and unjust court decisions. Through the performances by the landless peasants, Proshika realised that their initial plan of setting up economic projects such as fish farming or collective savings for the landless peasant would not achieve much within the existing power structures. Oppression at the grassroots was shown to involve a very complex system of collusion among the bureaucracy and state power. Meaningful change, therefore, called for a confrontation with these forces.

By 1980, therefore, Proshika committed itself to building up a movement of landless peasants that would mobilise many groups in a wider area for an effective struggle. From its experience with theatre, Proshika also realised that theatre was very well suited to the movement's need for mobilisation and conscientisation. Considering that the landless peasants were illiterate, the theatre was a better tool than print because it was a medium they could control both as performers and audience. It was, therefore, decided to make theatre an integral process of the peasant organisation.

Members of the *Aranyak* amateur theatre group were involved in conducting Popular Theatre workshops in the villages.

Kidd and Rashid[1] give a detailed account of the Proshika/ Aranyak Popular Theatre process. The team normally consists of five members and a co-ordinator. Each animateur is assigned to a specified village, within easy reach of the other animateurs' villages. The animateurs' work is co-ordinated by the co-ordinator, who provides information on what is happening all around and back-up support where it is needed. Each workshop goes through the stages of establishing a base in the village by living in the village, winning the confidence of the landless, listening to their problems, discussing and analysing the problems with the villagers, improvising scenarios together and changing them according to the villagers' views, holding a community performance during and after which there is a discussion with the audience and follow-up action.

As to the effectiveness of this Popular Theatre movement, Ahmed Faruque of Proshika gives one example:

> In Bangladesh the banks for giving rural credits are very corrupt. If you don't pay a certain amount you wont get loans and all this kind of thing. One Popular Theatre group in a village took up this issue. From all these people who had suffered from the process of taking loans, they got a story and presented it in the form of drama, performed it in front of the bank. What happened was that the bank was closed and the people from Dhaka came to investigate and the manager was sacked. So this has a power of exposing corruption and injustice and thereby sometimes preventing it. It is a tremendous power that popular theatre can have if it is linked with organisation-building.[2]

By 1984, Aranyak had run twenty-five workshops in about one hundred villages. Through this animation their work has had the impact of building up the people's capacity to run their own theatre performances and through that analyse their situation and thus start a more sustained process of conscientisation and organisation.

---

1. *Ibid.*
2. Faruque, A., 1987, "Empowerment in Action—Table Talk on Popular Theatre", *Adult Education Development and International Aid, Some Issues and Trends*, International Centre for Adult Education (compiled by Gunnar Rydström), Stockholm.

The Popular Theatre movement in Africa has received much inspiration from what has been happening in Latin America and Asia. There has even been some exchange of information and expertise especially through the International Popular Theatre Alliance, IPTA. Popular Theatre workers from Africa, Asia, and Latin America have, at times, had the opportunity to work together as was the case in a Bangladesh Proshika workshop and a workshop in Zimbabwe, both in 1983.

CHAPTER 4
The background to popular theatre in Africa

The theatre scene in Africa is very complex due to the heterogeneous nature of cultural traditions and the variety of historical factors that have shaped the function, form, and content of theatrical forms. African theatre practice displays a complex mixture—a coexistence of foreign, predominantly European dramatic genres and the indigenous dances, story-telling, mime and recitations.

Academic theory has for the past decade debated the existence and specific nature of African theatre. Some have even denied its existence.[1] Taban Lo Lyong states, for example, that, "there is nothing so culturally alien to Africa as the idea of theatre ... The dramatic re-enactment of historical events which often form part of religious festival involve acting but they are not meant as entertainment, nor have they produced a professional class of actors". Others have restricted African theatre to only those forms that are identical to European dramatic genre.[2] Today, however, there is general agreement that Africa has a distinct theatre based on her own cultural traditions. But what exactly constitutes African theatre is still a matter of debate. Theatre is here taken to include any performing art that represents life through symbolic images or artistic expressions that are in the form of action. The action can be in the form of dance, drama, mime, narration or a combination of any of these. Each society has its own theatre whose characteristics are shaped by its specific socio-economic structure. The background to theatre in Africa is best understood by dividing theatre into two major categories: the theatre of the dominant class, which is normally the minority, and that of the dominated majority.

---

1. Lyong, Taban Lo 1969, "The Role of the African Artist", in *Ghala, East African Journal*, Vol. VI, No. 1.
2. Hussein, E. 1975, *The Development of Drama in East Africa*, Ph.D. thesis, Humboldt University, Berlin.

In feudal or semi-feudal societies for example theatre existed to the entertainment of the royalty and were located at the courts. The heroic recitations of the Bahaya of Tanzania,[1] the Ankole of Uganda,[2] and the Tswana chiefs in Southern Africa[3] are some examples. These heroic recitations were used to foster the ideology of the ruling class and to maintain serfdom and servitude as the following example from the Bahaya in Tanzania illustrates:

> I am a tough character
> My soul is likened to a tobacco leaf
> My heart to a wooden spoon
> Which of the two is better
> It is you my lord the king who worries my mind
> I am totally committed to defending the kingdom
> I am among the survivors of Munene battle
> I carry my own food reserves in adventures
> I am the sorcerer of Lubwa
> I am a polygamist
> I grow fat after spending a night with a woman
> That is why I was given the praise name Nnenwe
> I prepared medicine for a leopard
> and hid it in the Ibembela forest
> Any leopard that crossed over it also drank it
> All leopards were killed after they had become mad
> Their skins were used to decorate the throne
> I was given the praise name Lubundazi
> A man who can take cover under cattle herds
> I am a tiger of the panther family
> Many attempts on my life have ended in vain
> I am the character you cannot easily bribe
> I side with good friends instead of a rich brother
> That is why I am trusted by kings
> That is why I was given the praise name Lukwekwe

---

1. Kazooba, B. 1975, *The Art of Recitation at a Bahaya King's Court*, mimeo, University of Dar es Salaam.
2. Morris, F. 1964, *The Heroic Recitations of the Bahima of Ankole*, Oxford University Press, Oxford.
3. Schapera, I. 1965, *Praise-Poems of Tswana Chiefs*, Oxford University Press, Oxford.

Lukwekwe implies my loyalty
cannot be distracted from the king
Whoever does wrong to my lord the king
will provoke my temper
And I will react ruthlessly like the Bwoe
spirit medium
Hail the sea that swallows rivers.[1]

The ruled, on the other hand, had their own theatre which dealt with issues and concerns of the popular classes including protests against their oppression under the feudal lords. The following is an example of a protest dance song against an exploitative chief from the Kaguru of Tanzania:

Mtemi Fulagobe	Chief tortoise
Haya Mtemi Fulagobe haya	Yes Chief tortoise
Mtemi ngholimaga	The chief never farms
Kadiaga fya wayagwe	All he does is eat off others' sweat.[2]

The European colonial rulers imposed European theatre on Africa. Their intention was not only to entertain the European community in the colonies but also to inculcate European values and attitudes among the colonised as part of the cultural domination crucial to the colonisation process. European dramatic theatre was introduced in the schools and "Little Theatres" were established in urban centres all over Africa.[3]

The indigenous theatre forms popular to the masses were either ignored or deliberately suppressed in the name of Christianity or civilisation. When an effort was made to promote the indigenous theatre forms there was often a colonisation intention behind it. For example, in 1948 the British colonial office introduced a policy that encouraged the performance of traditional dances in the colonies to brighten the lives of the people and thus distract them

---

1. Ishemoi, E. 1978, *The Heroic Recitations of the Bahaya of Bukoba*, mimeo, Department of Literature, University of Dar es Salaam.
2. Mlama, P. 1973, *Music in Tanzanian Traditional Theatre*, M.A. thesis, University of Dar es Salaam.
3. Hussein, E. *op. cit.*, and
   Traore, B. 1959, *The Black African Theatre and its Social Function*, (trans. D. Adelugba) Ibadan University Press, Ibadan.

from the mounting opposition to colonial domination in the empire.[1] Christian missionaries also used story-telling forms to preach Christianity by substituting the African mores with Christian teachings.[2]

Despite the hostile position of the colonial rulers, the indigenous forms flourished and became the rallying point for he protest against colonial domination. At times people defied the colonial administrators or settlers by ridiculing them in performances as was common in some Nigerian masquerades or the Ghanaian and Togolese Concert Party.[3] It was this potential for popular protest in the people's theatre which the liberation movements exploited in countries which had to resort to armed struggle. The Mau Mau in Kenya, Frelimo in Mozambique and ZANU in Zimbabwe used indigenous theatre forms not only to keep up the morale of their fighters but also to mobilise popular support among the masses. Zimbabwe's *Pungwe* is an outstanding example well summarised by Kidd who observes that:

> The war effort required an on-going dialogue with politicisation of and an active effort from the peasants. Long exhortatory speeches turned off the peasants. But when the speeches were shortened and combined with songs and dances, or when the same themes were conveyed through short sketches, the villagers responded with enthusiasm. When the villagers themselves became major actors and co-organisers of the event, their interest and support increased. The skits, songs, dance and poetry became an effective cover for the clandestine meetings and at the same time conveyed the ideas and spirit of revolution. It was highly participatory, villagers and fighters acted out and danced their commitments and built up their morale through collective music making.[4]

Unfortunately, the contribution of people's theatre to Africa's liberation from colonial domination is often understated or even completely ignored. Documentation of histories of struggles for independence in Africa often do not mention the artistic groups and individuals who through dance, song, poetry, recitations and

---

1. Tanzania National Archives, 1948, Reports of Group V Cambridge Summer Conference, TNA Secretarial file, 388/13.
2. White, P. 1950, *Jungle Doctor Fables*, Paternoster Press, London.
3. Kennedy, Scott 1973.
4. Kidd, R. 1986, *Popular Theatre: Conscientisation and Popular Organisation*, mimeo, Toronto.

such other forms played a significant role in mobilising people for the independence struggle. In Tanzania, for example, artists who played such a role include Kalikali, Mwinamila and Makongoro. But they are not mentioned in any of the books on the history of Tanzania's independence struggle.[1]

The ruling classes or post-independence Africa have patronised two major theatre movements. One is the neo-colonial theatre where European theatre practice is dominant. European plays, often irrelevant and unadapted to the African realities, are still staged in schools, universities and urban centres for the consumption of the elite. The British Council, the Goethe Institute or Alliance Française centres in African cities still lean towards promoting European theatre with the blessings of the host governments. For example, in 1986 the Goethe Institute in Nairobi sponsored the staging of three productions of unadapted and to a large extent irrelevant plays for children from the German Gripps Theatre repertoire. Jorg Friedrich, the director of the Gripps Theatre, was flown in to conduct a workshop for theatre artists from East Africa on how best to direct such plays. The three plays directed by Kenyans and acted by Kenyan children formed the basis of the workshop. It became very apparent during the workshop that both the directors and the actors only half understood what the plays were all about. The productions were mechanical reproductions of the scripts.

Secondly (as stated in chapter 1), some governments, having realised the potential that people's Popular Theatre had for mobilisation during the independence struggles, have decided to co-opt and domesticate that theatre in the interest of the ruling class. Under the banner of promoting national cultural identity indigenous theatre forms have been extensively used to propagate the ideology of the ruling class and to maintain the status quo. In Eastern and Southern Africa for example, dances by peasants pledging allegiance to official policies and praising the national leadership are a common sight. Tanzania is a good example of such a co-option of popular theatre forms. The Party (CCM) in collaboration with the ministries responsible for culture, has successfully mo-

---

1. See for example Ulotu, A. 1971, *Historia ya TANU*, East African Literature Bureau, Dar es Salaam.

bilised the people throughout the country to use their indigenous theatre forms to propagate *Ujamaa* policies. At present all significant Party functions from village to national level feature performances of dances, *ngonjera* (poetic drama) and music. The content of these performances is highly political but rarely expresses the genuine views and feelings of the artists. Instead, it is what the Party wants the audience to hear. Artists are usually supplied with themes relating to the Party occasion on which they should base their artistic compositions. In fact it is possible to trace the history of Party policies in Tanzania through the artistic repertoire. Similar trends are observable in Zimbabwe, Zambia, Kenya and Malawi.

Outside the state patronised theatre, though, the masses continue to perform their popular theatre forms which are a true expression of their own realities. In Tanzania, for example, besides the thousands of songs in support of the ruling ideology, one finds dance songs like the following:

> Alas for us drinkers
> They have closed our great pub
> But I must sue the government
> No mister, they want us to farm, friends
> So we can feed our children
> But we have always been great farmers
> I have already cultivated my rice farm
> And we still work on our farms.[1]

In Nigeria, the Kwang-hir puppetry among the Tiv was extensively used to protest against political victimisation in the 1960s.[2] Many more examples exist but are not recorded because such theatre lacks the official patronage that guarantees documentation through the official media.

The mass-based theatre forms are neglected by the ruling class for various reasons. The victims of capitalist cultural forces, mentioned earlier, see such theatre as part of the backward cultural heritage that needs to be dismissed as backward and anti-devel-

---

1. Mwakasaka, C. 1978, *The Oral Literature of the Banyakyusa*, Kenya Literature Bureau.
2. Kidd, R. 1982, "From Outside In to Inside Out; The Benue Workshop on Theatre for Development", *Theaterwork Magazine*, Vol. 2, No. 4, Toronto.

opment. It is true that many traditional theatre forms carry values and attitudes that are incompatible with the dynamics of contemporary society. However, dismissing the existence of this theatre totally, reflects a failure to understand the relationship between cultural expressions and a society's overall socio-economic structure. The fact that these indigenous forms are still active in many parts of rural Africa and in some cases expressing strong traditional values and attitudes points to their relevance to the existing structures that may not have changed as much as people think. Such theatre forms are a reflection of the fact that in spite of the pretense of development and modernity in urban areas, life for the majority has not changed much. The economic base is still characterised by underdevelopment of some elements of the pre-capitalist modes of production as a result of which its cultural superstructure portrays corresponding values and attitudes. To dismiss the cultural expressions without addressing the corresponding basic structure cannot result in development. On the other hand, such a view results from colonial hangover among the ruling class that makes them look upon rural cultural traditions as primitive.

In most cases though, the neglect of the mass-based theatre is a deliberate political decision predicated on the fear that promotion of ethnic cultures could jeopardise national integration efforts.[1] As Ajayi notes, "the nationalist leader attempting to rally the masses and re-establish their self-confidence by appealing to the cultural heritage soon realises that the more each cultural group takes pride in its own heritage the more difficult it is to achieve the common loyalty to a large political unity which is necessary for development".[2]

The more important fear, however, is for this theatre's potential to mobilise the masses to protest against injustice. Since most regimes have been characterised by corruption and exploitation of the masses, they always have a reason to fear opposition. Any-

---

1. See Ikiara, G. 1986, "State Policy on Culture and Economic Development: the Kenya Case", paper presented to the Regional Seminar on Culture and Economic Development, Arusha.
2. Ajayi, J. 1969, "The Place of African History and Culture in the Process of Nation Building in Africa, South of the Sahara", in Wallerstein (ed), *Social Change: the Colonial Situation*, Willey, New York.

thing with the power to raise the awareness of the masses is best left out. As Ngugi correctly points out:

> The theatre and the cinema are an expression of the drama in the lives of the people, that is an expression of their struggles, their conflicts, their hopes and fears. Their aspirations can make people view themselves positively and even be the beginning of an awakening of the slumbering powers within them. But unfortunately it is this very awakening of the slumbering powers within the people, indeed even the possibility of such an awakening which terrifies many of the ruling regimes in the Third World.[1]

It is clear to the ruling classes that the people's own theatre forms are not just an expression of outdated tribal feelings. Rather, some of these are the people's statements of discontent against corrupt, exploitative and unjust regimes. Given the chance, such theatre forms can successfully mobilise the masses against unpopular governments. The Kenyan government's reaction to the Kamiriithu theatre event in 1977, when peasants used their own theatrical expressions to portray Kenya's exploitative relations, is one example of the fear of the power of people's theatre by ruling systems. In Kamiriithu, the centre which hosted the organisation of the peasant's theatre was closed down, the theatre building erected voluntarily by the villagers was razed to the ground and some of the leaders of the production arrested or forced to flee the country.[2] The Kamiriithu case is discussed in more detail in Chapter 5.

Censorship boards in many African countries have also stalled the development of progressive mass-based theatre movements while the non-extension of material and moral state support has constantly frustrated individual attempts at such theatre practice.

As such, the mass-based popular theatre forms have been pushed to the background. This is the inevitable fate of the culture of dominated classes which, corresponding to their economic and political subjugation, is bound to be dominated by the culture of the dominant classes. Such domination though, has not led to the

---

1. Ngugi wa Thiong'o 1982, "Women in Cultural Work: the Fate of Kamiriithu People's Theatre—Kenya", *Development Dialogue*, Vol. 1–2, The Dag Hammarskjöld Foundation, Uppsala.
2. Kidd, R. 1983, "Popular Theatre and Popular Struggle in Kenya: The Story of Kamiriithu", *Race and Class*, Vol. XXIV, 3.

elimination of the popular theatre tradition. People continue to use their dances, mimes, drama, recitations and story-telling to express their views about their realities, to discuss their problems, to air their fears and aspirations, to condemn and protest against injustice, even though most of it goes unheeded by the powers that be.

The contemporary Popular Theatre movement in Africa is a continuation of this long tradition of theatre. It is not, as is often claimed,[1] an innovation of the 1960s when the university-based theatre artists embarked on a search for a mass-based theatre practice. Instead, it is an attempt to bring to the fore a long tradition that has constantly been overshadowed by the dominant classes.

The emergence of the contemporary Popular Theatre movement was prompted by a number of factors. The 1960s were the years of the search for cultural identity. One of the tasks of independent states was the reassertion of their cultural identity which the colonial rulers had tried to eradicate.[2] The elite theatre artists set out to contribute towards this ideal by researching into the Africa theatre heritage and reviving through various theatre experiments the indigenous theatre forms which the Europeans had termed savage and uncivilised. The incorporation of African music, dances, poetry, costume, scenery, myths and legends in the university theatre production of the 1960s was the response. Wole Soyinka, J.P. Clark, Efua Sutherland, Ama Ata Aidoo, Okot p'Bitek, and Bob Leshoai are some of the advocates of that theatre practice. The universities of Ibadan (Nigeria), Legon (Ghana), Makerere (Uganda), Dar es Salaam (Tanzania), and Lusaka (Zambia) were the more active in that movement. Many playwrights also emerged who used African themes and settings to produce an African version of the hitherto predominantly European drama. Ibrahim Hussein, Ngugi wa Thiong'o, Wole Soyinka, and John Ruganda are a few examples of the forerunners of such playwrights.

---

1. See Byram, Martin et al. 1981, *The Report of the Workshop for Integrated Development*, Department of Extra Mural Studies, University of Swaziland, and Etherton, M. 1982, *The Development of African Drama*, Hutchinson, London.
2. See Ngugi wa Thiong'o 1986.

The call by politicians for national cultural revival also brought about the emergence of semi-professional commercial theatre movements based on popular indigenous theatrical expressions. The Concert Party and the Nigerian Folk Opera reached their zenith in the 1960s. Meanwhile, many governments were proving their commitment to their national cultures by establishing national dance troupes whose appearance at state functions, especially at airports during state visits, became fashionable. The Ugandan Heart Beat of Africa and the Guinean Joliba are memorable examples. In their own way the masses in the rural areas also felt encouraged to perform their dances without fear of the priest who previously might have threatened them with excommunication from the church.

These early efforts contributed significantly towards giving the Africans pride in their own culture which colonisation had made them feel ashamed of. They also helped to prop up the political feelings of liberation from colonial rule and a sense of belonging to a nation that had respect for African things. The more progressive theatre artists, however, were soon disturbed by the parading of middle-class urban-based theatre movements as examples of "African culture". It became apparent that the experiments at universities, the national dance troupes and the commercial enterprises only catered for a minority. Thus began the Travelling Theatre movement by such African universities as those at Makerere, Dar es Salaam, Ibadan, and Lusaka.

The Travelling Theatre was based on the concept of taking theatre to the people. Recognising the economic deprivation of the rural masses, the urban elite felt obliged to assist in transmitting development to the people not only through the construction of schools, health centres, and water pumps but also by taking theatre to the villages. University-based theatre groups prepared productions at their campuses and tried to come up with plays based on African themes, at times even using the local languages of the intended audiences. They then took the productions on a tour of the rural areas where, adapting to the local conditions of no theatre buildings or electricity, they performed before village audiences. Many such performances were received with a lot of enthusiasm especially when the themes were recognisable to the audiences or when the local languages were the medium. The villagers who were used to being despised by the city-dwelling elite were fascinated by the elite's realisation of the importance of coming to the village to share experiences.

Various shortcomings of the Travelling Theatre concept have, however, been noted. First, is the assumption implicit in the idea of "taking theatre to the people" that those people do not have a theatre of their own. Travelling Theatre represented an imposition of outsiders' agendas and analysis. One is reminded of what Cabral observes of undemocratic and non-participatory processes of development. In Travelling Theatre, too, the peasants were left out of the action, forced into the conventional role of watching someone else's interpretation of the reproduction of their culture of silence. "They remained the passive recipients of outside ideas, robbed of an opportunity to voice their own concerns, to do their own thinking."[1] Second, the Travelling Theatre was embarking on a futile venture to spread a middle-class type of theatre among the peasantry. The objectives was to influence the people to start similar groups all over the country. It did not strike these theatre artists that this was an impossible task due to the alien nature of that theatre and the lack of a base for its possible development. Theatre emerges out of a people's way of life and not from a one day show by a visiting group.

The Travelling Theatre also leaned more towards the provision of entertainment, emulating the bourgeoisie theatre from which it emerged. Like the urban-based theatre movements, it did not bring out the more significant ideological functions of theatre. Little effort was made to use the potential for the theatre to analyse problems and to offer criticism. This was contrary to the character of the popular theatre forms in the villages which normally combine entertainment with education and critical analysis.

Although the Travelling Theatre approach is still in practice in some parts of Africa today, the more progressive theatre artists abandoned it in the 1970s for a new approach referred to as Theatre for Development and more recently Popular Theatre.

Popular Theatre refers to the employment of a variety of theatrical expressions at grassroot level to research and analyse development problems and to create a critical awareness and poten-

---

1. Cabral, Amilcar 1973.

tial for action to solve those problems. Popular Theatre may be seen as an effort to develop a type of theatre that is relevant to people's life and struggle as opposed to the theatre of entertainment and abstraction from reality of the dominant classes. Here theatre is used not only to develop theatre as a form of cultural expressions but also, and more significantly, as a tool for improving life in its totality. Theatre becomes a process through which man studies and forms an opinion about his environment, analyses it, expresses and shares his viewpoint about it and acquires the frame of mind necessary for him to take action to improve upon it. As such, theatre is economic, social, political—indeed life itself.

The next chapter traces the Popular Theatre movement in Africa from the 1970s to the present. Emphasis is placed on posing Popular Theatre as a practical example of the use of theatre as an ideological tool thus promoting the integration of culture into a people's development process.

CHAPTER 5

The popular theatre movement in Africa from the 1970s

The continent of Africa is subjected to oppressive and exploitative forces very similar to the situation in Asia and Latin America. Colonialism, capitalism, and imperialism have systematically impoverished Africa, plunging most of her countries into a crisis whose economic, political, social, and cultural complexity make the future very bleak. As mentioned in Chapter 1, Africa, together with other developing countries, is getting poorer. The alliance of most of the national ruling classes with international capital to exploit the rest of the people has not helped the situation. Today the masses in Africa are much more aware than they were in the wake of independence in the 1960s of the fact that their fellow countrymen in the seats of power are only interested in grabbing power. People are witnessing the ludicrous amassing of wealth, mostly through illegal means by those who, on political platforms, have promised a better life for all. Indeed, the fruits of independence seem to have bypassed the majority, and their continued efforts are still needed to free themselves from the numerous forces of their exploitation.

This crisis has created fertile ground in Africa for the consolidation of the Popular Theatre tradition discussed in Chapter 4, and its use as a tool in the struggle against the forces undermining people's welfare. A Popular Theatre movement has emerged in Africa as a conscious effort to assert the culture of the dominated classes. It attempts to create a way of life where people at the grassroot level are aware of the forces at work in determining their living conditions. It aims to make the people not only aware of but also active participants in the development process by expressing their viewpoints and acting to better their conditions. Popular Theatre is intended to empower the common man with a critical consciousness crucial to the struggles against the forces responsible for his poverty. It is an attempt to enable the masses to break free from the culture of silence imposed on them and reawaken or strengthen their latent culture of resistance and struggle, which needs to be part of the process to bring about their development.

This chapter outlines the Popular Theatre movement from the 1970s to the present. Since Africa is a large continent with a wide variety of theatre practice, it is not possible to cover all countries. Instead, the focus is on those countries whose approaches to Popular Theatre present the major models characterising the Popular Theatre movement in Africa. These countries include Malawi, Botswana, Swaziland, Lesotho, Zambia, Sierra Leone, Nigeria, Zimbabwe, Cameroon, Kenya, and Tanzania. It ought to be mentioned here, too, that this study does not include the French-speaking African countries due to the fact that material on the subject have been inaccessible to the author.

The Popular Theatre movement in contemporary Africa has followed several different approaches with varying degrees of success in the realisation of its goals. For example, a populist form of theatre, often incorrectly referred to as Popular Theatre, has existed in many parts of Africa. It is based on a "developmentalist" approach, whereby popular theatre forms are used to carry development messages to an audience which is expected to translate those messages into action. For example, a play exhorts the farmers to adopt modern farming methods or villagers to build latrines, boil drinking water or learn literacy skills. This type of theatre is a carry-over of the practices of the British colonial government which used this approach in countries like Ghana or Malawi. As Kamlongera says: "As early as in the 1930s, colonial health workers, secondary school teachers, agricultural and community extension workers, were using drama to sell the virtues of modernisation, cash crop productivity, and financial prudence."[1] Field workers travelled from village to village organising drama performances, discussions and demonstrations based on such campaign topics as cash crop production, taxation, and disease

---

1. Kamlongera, C. 1986, *Puppet Theatre in Malawi's Ministry of Agriculture: an Example of Extension Services in Agriculture,* paper presented to the Regional Seminar on Culture and Economic Development, Arusha.

eradication. The theatrical programmes were planned, messages chosen, and scripts prepared by government extension workers. The early post-independence years saw some governments continuing the same approach in a bid to use theatre as a tool for development. In 1964 through its Extension Aids Section, the Malawi Ministry of Agriculture initiated the use of puppetry for agricultural extension work.[1] The Section employs a full-time technical assistant whose duty is to make puppets. An agricultural officer prepares the scripts on the basis of major agricultural campaign activities in the target areas. The scripts are also accompanied by popular music. Kamlongera describes the puppet show as follows:

> Equipped with three puppets, recordings of some dramatised agricultural message, music and a land-rover specially fitted with a puppet stage and loudspeaker at the back, a team of puppet operators go to the field to do their work ... Popular music is played through loudspeakers to attract the attention of would-be audiences until a sizeable group collects. A local extension worker introduces the puppet play and summarises its message after it has come to an end. When the play has been introduced, the puppet operator takes his position behind the stage. The recorded dialogue is then played through loudspeakers whilst the puppet operator moves puppets at appropriate times to indicate which character is speaking. Throughout the entire show the operator remains hidden behind the stage built at the back of the land-rover.[2]

From such performances, the audiences were expected to adopt the advocated agricultural practices and thus increase production.

Even though one could mistake this type of theatrical venture for Popular Theatre because of its preoccupation with people at grassroot level and its use of theatrical forms popular with the people, it is important to note that such theatre is not truly popular. It is, in fact, an invasion from above. The villagers are treated as depositories, or to use Freire's term "empty pots", for propaganda containing messages which exclude their own viewpoints. The large audiences reached by these theatre programmes may be entertained by the shows, some of which do become popular, but they are passive recipients of a content over which they have no control. Commenting on a similar programme in Ghana Kidd

---

1. Kerr, D. 1981, "An Experiment in Popular Theatre in Malawi: The University Travelling Theatre's Visit to Mbalachanda, Chancellor College".
2. Kamlongera, C.

points out that "the programme operates in a one-way banking fashion with the organisers imposing their views of what people need ... and I ought to know in order to become modern".[1] The same could be said of the LEARN (Local Educational Activities of Rural Networks) programme in Sierra Leone, conducted by CARE between 1979 and 1983. LEARN used taped dramatised stories featuring the experiences of a typical rural family to transmit development messages on agriculture, health, nutrition, and sanitation.[2]

The shortcomings of this approach became apparent, and in the mid-1970s a search for a Popular Theatre approach that would involve the participation of target audiences was initiated. It was also felt that the extension approach to development then in practice reinforced the one-way, top-down system of communication for development. "The extension networks tended to be more concerned with providing services and information, rather than encouraging people's participation in development. Often the messages conveyed by the extension workers were externally conceived rather than based on an assessment of local needs. Theatre, used in a participatory way, seemed to offer an alternative way of overcoming apathy and addressing some of the more pressing local problems,"[3] as a report stated. The extension workers themselves were in many areas also in search of an approach to development that would bring about better results.

Kidd observes that in Botswana adult educators and extension workers had a feeling of inadequacy in dealing with the severe problems faced by rural poverty, unemployment, poor health, and community and family disintegration. They realised that they could make very little impact on agriculture, health or community problems without beginning with an analysis of the larger social forces controlling their situation.[4]

---

1. Kidd, R. 1983, "From Outside In to Inside Out; The Benue Workshop on Theatre for Development", *Media in Education and Development*, March.
2. Malamah, D. 1986, *Innovative Community Theatre for Integrated Rural Development in Sierra Leone: the Tellu Workshop Experience* (unpublished), Fourah Bay.
3. Byram, M. et al. 1981, "The Report of the Workshop for Integrated Development", Department of Extra Mural Studies, University of Swaziland.
4. Kidd, R. 1979, "Liberation or Domestication—Popular Theatre and Non-Formal Education in Africa", *Educational Broadcasting International*, March.

The *Laedza Batanani* Popular Theatre programme in Botswana was born out of this argument. *Laedza Batanani* was an adult education programme started in 1974 as an integrated community education campaign. It was an annual one week event during which a team of actors toured the villages putting on performances and organising discussions on the highlighted issues. The performances were, however, preceded by the attendance of community representatives at a pre-campaign planning workshop in which priority issues were identified. Local councillors provided the overall leadership of the campaigns. Extension workers in the area were also involved as local organisers of community participation. During the performance tour, the team covered five major villages. In each village they put on a one and a half hour performance, including drama, puppetry, dance, song and drumbeat poetry. After each performance, the actors and other extension workers in the area divided the audience into groups and organised discussions of the problems presented. A discussion started with an objective look at the problems as they affect the members of the audience and what might be done about them.

The topics for the performances in the first four years of *Laedza Batanani* included cattle theft, inflation, unemployment, the effect on community and family of migrant labour, conflicts between traditional and modern practices, education and health problems.[1]

The *Laedza Batanani* model introduced a two-way communication process important in development communication. People were made aware of their situation, encouraged to look at their problems and take action to solve them instead of merely accepting messages from government employees. Assessing this programme, Kidd, one of its organisers, observes that:

> It has led people to question openly the practices of specific individuals and institutions e.g. theft by the treasurer of the village development committee, indecision by government regarding assistance to a flooded village, corruption by a headman who had been imposed on a minority tribal group, exploitation of cattle-workers etc. Poorer villagers, women, and others who had been unable to express their opinions in the village meetings have started to become more vocal about various forms of op-

---

1. Byram, M. *et al.*

pression e.g. bad treatment by clinic staff, the heavy workloads of women and so on.[1]

The considerable success of the *Laedza Batanani* approach was soon to influence similar programmes in Swaziland, Lesotho, Zambia, and Malawi. A Zambian programme took the form of two workshops, the first one being the Theatre for Development Workshop held in Chalimbana in 1979 followed by another workshop in 1981 specifically on the use of theatre for primary health care. For Zambia this was a shift from the University of Zambia's Chikwakwa Travelling Theatre approach. The shortcomings of the travelling theatre approach pointed out in Chapter 4, made the *Laedza Batanani* model more appealing to both development agents and theatre workers.

In the Chalimbana workshop, theatre and development workers came together to generate ideas on using theatre as a tool for development. The participants included theatre workers from Southern and East Africa. They worked with five villages and produced skits on themes identified and discussed by the villagers involved. The skits were staged in the villages, sparking off extensive discussion with the audiences. The 1981 workshop concerned with primary health was conducted along similar lines.

In Swaziland, a programme was effected through a National Workshop for Integrated Development held in Nhlango in 1981. Initiated by the Division of Extra Mural Services of the University College of Swaziland in collaboration with the ministries of Health, Education and Agriculture and Co-operatives, the workshop was basically designed to train extension workers in the use of theatre for development. The organisers believed that theatre offered a promising break-through in communication for development. In the words of the Director of the Extra Mural Services Division:

> The more established means and methods of communication have not succeeded in reaching those people in the rural areas: some cannot read, others cannot afford radio and television sets and in most cases, they cannot be reached by radio and television. Theatre, on the other hand, has been used as yet another new method of reaching a majority of peo-

---

1. Kidd, R. 1983.

ple. It has also been used to enable those affected to be actively involved in their own educational process.[1]

After their information gathering in the target villages, the participants, extension and theatre workers, rehearsed and put on performances in the villages. One of these was a dance drama with the following storyline:

> It is a family scene. The mother is fetching water, the husband is working in the fields, and the boy is herding the cows. Meanwhile the head of another family is drinking at the local *shebeen* with his friends when his son comes to tell him his child is sick. He rushes home and then goes to get help with the Rural Development Aid. The husband arrives with the RDA (Rural Development Authority) vehicle and the family drives off to the clinic, but they fail to cross the river. The wife and child return home whilst the husband tries to cross and reach the clinic but he is attacked by two murderers. He escapes and returns home. They decide to wait for the bus the following day ... During the night, the woman of the other family falls sick with diarrhoea. The next morning both the families catch the bus but it cannot cross the river and they have to walk the rest of the way. The sick woman dies almost as soon as she arrives at the clinic. The doctor certifies her death and the distressed husband carries his wife away with the help of his friends. The family with the sick child is seen by the doctor ...
>
> A meeting is called by the chief. He sends a messenger to call the people, the RDA Manager and the clinic staff. When they arrive the chief addressed the people about the complaints he had heard on the death of the sick woman, the distance to the clinic, the poor bridges, the presence of murderers and general conditions in the community. The people agree that something needs to be done and under the guidance of the chief, they start to work and sing. As they sing, they begin to build the clinic, dig the toilets and construct a bridge.[2]

Using also drama and puppetry, the participants put on other performances covering a wide range of problems identified in the area. These problems included resettlement, illiteracy, land shortage, unsuccessful co-operatives, bad village leadership, bad health conditions, unavailability of social amenities, unemployment, and alcoholism.

Inspired by the colonial heritage of using theatre for extension work and the University Travelling Theatre's attempt at finding closer links with rural audiences, Malawi launched a Theatre for

---

1. Byram, M. *et al.*
2. *Ibid.*

Development workshop in Mbalachanda rural growth centre in 1981. Under the auspices of the University of Malawi, the University Travelling Theatre Group decided to improve on its continuing travelling theatre approach by addressing the problems of the rural audiences. The Mbalachanda workshop, therefore, involved extension workers at Mbalachanda in the creation of plays to illustrate some of the problems which extension workers were trying to deal with in the community ground.

Mbalachanda, one of the "Rural Growth Centres" had been built with West German technical assistance. It was meant to create a focal point of development in the underdeveloped areas of Malawi by providing social and economic services, contributing to the decentralisation of administration and giving rural people an opportunity to better participate in development activities as well as enabling the integration of development activities in the rural areas. It was felt, therefore, that a theatre for development workshop would enhance such objectives.[1]

Due to inadequate time and the need for special permission, the group could not, however, conduct the information gathering process through which they could involve the villagers in collecting and discussing the data on the problems concerned. Instead, a discussion was held with extension officers and on the basis of that discussion, plays were created by the University group on the themes of illiteracy, bad sanitation and cultural resistance to agriculture extension work. It is not surprising that the four plays resulting from this workshop were developmentalist, emphasising the view of the extension officers. They fitted Kerr's criticism of Malawian "Theatre for Development" in which he argues that the plays, rather than analysing problems, simply castigate the poor for their ignorance. The archetypal developmentalist play shows a caricature of a traditional villager routinely defeated by the equally stock figure of an enlightened progressive farmer/health worker/community development officer. The following storyline of one of the Mbalachanda plays serves as an example:

> Two couples, the Mkandawires and the Bandas, count their money after selling tobacco to the tobacco farm manager of their estate. They have both earned the same amount from the sales. The primary school teacher

---

1. Kerr, D. 1981.

who is in charge of "Kwacha" literacy classes calls a meeting of tenant farmers and their wives. He explains about "kwacha" schools and answers their questions. Mr and Mrs Banda and Mrs Mkandawire enroll for literacy classes but Mr Mkandawire refuses on the ground that they are unmanly and impractical. Mr Mkandawire becomes suspicious of his wife's activities when he sees the male teacher guiding her hand with the writing. Mr Mkandawire sulks at home when his wife returns from school. He is a little mollified when his son confirms that his wife has acquired some basic reading, writing and numeracy skills. A scene at the end-of-harvest money counting similar to the opening in which the Bandas gloat over the Mkandawires because Mr Banda has earned more than Mkandawire for tobacco sales, owing to Banda's improved numeracy skills. Mkandawire storms off furiously.[1]

Malawian theatre, however, breaks out of this narrow concept of theatre for development with the 1987 Liwonde project discussed later in this chapter.

Lesotho also adopted the *Laedza Batanani* for their earlier work with the Maratholli Travelling Theatre between 1982 and 1985. Organised by the National University of Lesotho's department of English and the Institute of Extra Mural Studies, the programme produced plays covering such themes as reforestation, co-operatives and rehabilitation of prisoners. Horn outlines the story of one such play:

> The situation explored was that of a village, where the farmers were alarmed by the rate of infant deaths. A rural primary health care worker is invited to speak and explain the need for maintaining the cleanliness of wells and streams. But one family, owners of sizable herds of cattle and sheep, objects to covering the wells because their livestock would then have to be driven further to drink. The other villagers, however, proceed to fashion the necessary structures out of the available materials (local stones, discarded roofing materials, thatching grass). Shortly after, the antagonist's baby sickens and dies. The father is convinced that, given his neighbour's hostility, the child has been bewitched. But a relative arrives for the funeral and tells the farmer that in a nearby village similar deaths had occurred as a result of a typhoid outbreak halted only by the building of pit latrines and well covers. The antagonists eventually join the rest of the community in support of the sanitation campaigns.[2]

A group of students normally went out to the villages and gathered information on the problems of the target areas. Then they

---
1. *Ibid.*
2. *Ibid.*

analysed and prioritised the information on the basis of which they improvised stories, rehearsed and staged them at the villages. A post-performance discussion would be held with the audience and extension workers. Follow-up action in the form of practical advice to the villagers on how to go about solving the portrayed problems was also added.

Lesotho, however, soon dropped the *Laedza Batanani* approach for reasons which also led the later Popular Theatre attempts to abandon this model. Zakes Mda, one of the organisers of Maratholi explains:

> We have now completely discarded this method for we feel that, if the message is pre-packaged, the process does not differ much from the top-down communication that we are so much against. To us it seemed as though through our research in the villages people told us their problems, and through our theatre we "solved" their problems. In other words this kind of theatre is geared towards persuasion to influence people to do what we think is right for them, instead of trying to raise the level of their critical awareness so that they may examine and find ways of solving their problems themselves. Indeed there are post performance discussions, but we discovered that in many cases such discussions lead to individual action on a short term basis, a discovery which tallies with other experiences in various parts of the world where this method has been a medium of development communication.[1]

It has been pointed out that the *Laedza Batanani* approach, indeed, does not make theatre authentically popular in the sense of theatre being the people's own communication medium. As Kidd writes:

> The villagers are not involved in the process of analysing the information, scripting the drama and performing the plays. The extension workers collect the villager's information and then retreat to analyse the data and work out a performance on their own. This lack of participation severly reduces the commitment of the villagers by disengaging them from the crucial aspects of the process. Without the villagers' involvement in the analysis and drama making process, the exension workers are forced to fall back on their own stereotyped thinking and analysis, which often reduces complex social problems to a matter of villagers' ignorance, apathy, or bad habits. While the day of research is meant to open up field workers' eyes to challenge their assumptions, to force them to listen to the villagers, it often serves to reinforce their prejudices, and without a continuing encounter with the villagers and the village reality there is

---

1. Horn, A. 1984, "Public Health, Public Theatre—a Report from Southern Africa", *Medicine and Society*, X, 1–2, London.

little room for challenging these prejudices. The discussion at the end of the performance is too brief to achieve anything more than a superficial analysis of the problems, let alone strategise for action. After passively watching the play, the villagers are suddenly expected to discuss the problems and take action.[1]

The Maratholi programme, therefore, has instead adopted what they refer to as Theatre for Conscientisation, discussed later in this chapter.

The Nigerian Ahmadu Bello University (ABU) Theatre group came up with an improved approach through their rural theatre workshops in the Bomo area in 1981. The Bomo workshop was a step ahead of ABU's previous theatre for development that operated on the same lines as the Southern Africa experiences. The 1977 *Wason Manoma*, (farmers' plays), for example, were designed to support the national food campaign. The ABU group researched into the major agricultural problems by consulting agricultural experts and talking to farmers. From that information they improvised and staged plays on such topics as the arrogance and ignorance of agricultural experts from the cities, migration to towns, or corruption of government officials and village leaders in the distribution of fertilizers. The 1979 Maska workshop also dealt with literacy, health and hygiene, and involved adult literacy officers from Northern Nigerian states.

After the Maska workshop, ABU reports that they were by then very conscious that their work had failed to involve the villagers except as an essentially passive audience who could briefly make comments after the performance. It was the desire to remedy this situation that prompted ABU to take up the Bomo workshop. The Bomo approach involved an emphasis on improvisation and the repeated revision of the drama in the light of constant debate. Instead of staging a finished play and asking the audience to discuss it at the end, only rough skits were started and then frequently stopped to allow the audience to contribute to what should follow next or to improvise on what should follow next or to improvise on what had been done by giving comments or actually taking part as actors.

---

1. Mda, Z. 1987, "Towards an Alternative Perspective of Development", *Union of African Performing Artists Newsletter*, Yaounde, No. 16, November.

The ABU model was in fact patterned on the Augusto Boal theatre methodology, sometimes referred to as Forum Theatre in which theatre is essentially a process of liberation through which the audience is actively involved in a critical analysis of what is presented.

The following is an account of one performance by ABU, using this approach:

> Each scene required village participation: our own team members played the bureaucrats but all the other roles were assigned to the villagers. They took up their roles very easily and added much more depth to the discussion of the issues in the play. For example, in the village co-op meeting scene, one of the villagers spontaniously raised the issue of bribing the government store official (as a possible strategy) and another expressed his disgruntlement with the co-op and demanded his membership fee back. Another villager in this meeting accused the co-op representative of "chopping" (misappropriating) the members' money.
>
> At the end of the fertilizer scene we stopped and asked for their reaction. One man said we had not shown how people wait for days in the queue outside the government store. So we replayed the government store scene under his direction, creating a huge line-up (made of the villagers), lots of shoving and jockeying for position within the line, the storekeeper ignoring people in the line and keeping everyone waiting, the trader being challenged by the farmers when he tried to jump the queue, the whole line bursting into the storekeeper's office when they overheard the trader bribing the storekeeper, and the agricultural officer eventually driving the farmers out of the store.[1]

In this approach the core actors still come from outside the community. In this one, the team was driving to the village and back everyday of the workshop. They also rehearsed their introductory skits at the workshop centre away from the village. The participatory nature of the performance, however, allows the members of the community to actively debate issues, present their point of view even by actually becoming the actors and in the process raising their consciousness and critical awareness of their reality.

This is the approach that later characterised the work of the Maratholi group mentioned earlier. The Liwonde Primary Health Care Unit with the assistance of the Chancellor College Fine and Performing Arts Department in Malawi used the same process to actively involve the Mwima and Mbela villagers in primary health

---

1. Kidd, R. 1983.

care. Initiated in 1986, the major concern for the Liwonde PHC project was how to ensure community participation. Experiences in Malawi and elsewhere had shown that a primary health care or any other social welfare project has little chance of success if it does not allow people to make their own decisions and take their own actions. Popular Theatre was, therefore, incorporated into the Primary Health Care (PHC) programme for the purpose of effecting community participation.

The PHC Team, a theatre team, and the villagers worked together to discuss health problems, research into their causes and take action to solve them. The theatre performance is described by Chris Kamlongera, the organiser, as follows:

> The play that was presented was a mixture of drama and open discussion. A mother comes to complain to her chief before his elders that she has lost her son in a drowning accident. Further discussion of the accident leads to a decision that the villagers should dig a well from which they can draw water instead of using the river which is not only dangerous but infested with all sorts of diseases.
>
> Having agreed that they should have a well, another problem comes up. Where do they site the well? The chief dictates that it should be close to his house, but the elders object and suggest alternative sites which are also objectionable. One is too close to the graveyard and therefore culturally unacceptable. The other one is too far although at the centre of the shopping area. The chief then opens the debate to other villagers present (the audience) to express their views on the subject. At this point the play becomes a real discussion rather than just entertainment. The villagers join in the debate.
>
> They point out that a well close to the chief's house will inevitably be difficult to approach at will as the chief will expect people to treat it as if it was his personal property. Their choice happens to be somewhere in the middle of the village.
>
> The discussion moves on to touch on how the village should actually take care of the well once it is dug, what people should not do in order to make it clean. Most articulate in this part of the discussion/drama are women for they are more knowledgeable about usage of wells than men. Several problems related to the question of water are brought out. At this point the theatre group opens the participation in the dramatisation to the villagers by encouraging the latter to act in a repeat of the sketch just presented, but incorporating the ideas and arguments that came along as

it was first performed. In this way, more arguments, discussion on the issues relevant to the question of the well and its maintenance evolve.[1]

Kamlongera goes on to note that as a result of the incorporation of Popular Theatre the PHC programmes in Mbela and Mwima have been quite successful. The village health committees have been very active resulting in the protection of over forty shallow wells, and 51 per cent of the households had constructed pit latrines as compared to 10 per cent a year earlier. Awareness of general health practices is felt to be higher than before the programme.

In 1983, a workshop on Theatre for Development was held in Murewa, Zimbabwe. The broad aims of the workshop included the training of theatre workers, development cadres and local villagers in the skill and process of theatre for conscientisation and mobilisation. Bringing together artists from different parts of Africa, the workshop was located in the Murewa district, seven villages of which were involved in the process.

Murewa is basically an agricultural area with a population of about 350,000. Its socio-economic conditions bear witness to some of the problems that Zimbabwe is facing in constructing a newly independent state after a long war of liberation from white colonial settlers' domination. The land available to Africans is both poor and inadequate. Most of the young people are, therefore, forced to flock into the towns in search of employment. The Murewa town has a large population of such people. Many of the unemployed are also the ex-freedom fighters, thousands of whom await rehabilitation and resettlement through governmental programmes. Although these have been introduced, their implementation is both slow and costly. Underdevelopment characterises the villages which have largely served as labour reserves. The ravages of a long war of liberation are also visible in various social and cultural manifestations.

The Murewa workshop was fashioned much on the ABU model. Participants (theatre artists, extension workers, and some bureaucrats) stayed at a workshop centre in Murewa growth point and drove back and forth from the seven surrounding villages in groups. The process included information gathering by the team

---

1. Kalipeni, E. and C. Kamlongera 1987, *Popular Theatre and Health Care*, Chancellor College, Malawi, (unpublished).

with the assistance of some local liaisons. Then followed rehearsals based on improvisations by the participants and performances at the village followed by a discussion with the audience. Several groups managed to improve on the ABU approach by situating their theatrical work at the village with a considerable active participation of the members of the community. It was interesting to note that in some cases the workshop team was forced to create together with the villagers because of a very active artistic tradition in Zimbabwe which the workshop team had underestimated. As mentioned in Chapter 1, artistic expression had played a very significant role in the war of liberation. Artistic expression, especially dance and songs are, therefore, very much alive and at the fingertips of most of the Zimbabwe rural population. As one of the workshop team members reports:

> We started off with an exchange of songs ... This set the right spirit and inspired the village women who simply took over the session and turned it into a spontaneous celebration. The tremendous outpouring of songs, dances and games showed that we would have no trouble getting the villagers to participate. If anything, we would need to shake a leg, several legs, to match their spirit! The villagers saw that they had relevant skills and experience to contribute and that their ideas and performances were crucial to the process. It showed we could achieve a genuine dialogue and collaboration, with initiative coming as much from them as from us.[1]

In another group, the villagers took over the show and dramatised their problems of isolation due to the lack of a bridge and inaction caused by alcoholism.

The following is a description of the work of the group, in which the author participated. Our group included some twenty members and our area of operation was the Murewa growth point, a semi-urban and administrative centre of the district. It is a trading centre with a market, shops and an excessive number of liquor stores. A good road connects Murewa to other parts of the country.

The first stage of the work was information gathering, covering as much of the growth point area as possible. A long list of problems was produced, but the major ones centred around the influx of the unemployed youth to the centre from the surrounding ar-

---

1. Kidd, R. 1986.

eas. Many of the youth were ex-combatants of the recently ended war of liberation. Delinquency, violence and loitering were on the increase. The uncontrolled liquor business led to excessive drinking, prostitution, and an alarming spread of venereal diseases. The District council, most of whose members were the owners of the liquor stores, did not seem to be effective in handling these problems.

Using Zimbabwean traditional dances, including the famous Jerusalema, the group improvised a dance drama with the following storyline:

The drama starts at the village. There is a large family with a very small piece of land. The father has to stay in Harare where he has a very low paying job. One son leaves home and goes to the Murewa growth point in search for a job. At the growth point there are many other young boys and girls looking for jobs, too. The boy and a girl from his village go to a liquor store to seek employment. Because of her looks and therefore the potential to attract customers, the possibility of sexual benefits for the employer, and the lower wages paid to girls than to boys, the girl is offered a job and not the boy. After much hardship, the boy turns pick-pocketing and joins a gang of other unemployed boys. They terrorise the growth centre, one of their victims being a district councillor. After some time the girl becomes the girlfriend of her employer, who is also a district councillor.

Then there is a councillors' meeting. The councillor/bar owner comes to the meeting but it is obvious that he is suffering from VD which he has picked from the bar maid (the girl). The agenda for the meeting included the economic and social welfare of the growth centre, the large number of unemployed youth, the many liquor stores, and uncontrolled petty trade. Because of different class interests, the councillors do not agree on many issues. For example, one councillor wants certain bars closed down because they are a health hazard but the councillors who themselves own bars refuse. Another one supports the idea but basically because he wants to allocate that business to his friend. Eventually, the council decides to start economic youth brigades as a means of opening up economic opportunities for the unemployed.

Back at the village the mother is struggling with the younger children. She brews *kachasu*, an illicit liquor, in order to survive.

The boy comes back to his mother because he has contracted VD in the town and is too shy to go to the clinic. He drinks his mother's *kachasu* which people believe cures VD. But he gets very sick and the mother is very angry with this useless son. Relatives intervene and send the boy to the clinic. At the clinic, he is subjected to the problems of clinic queues and lack of personnel. Other youth from the growth centre also come to the clinic with different diseases all related to their social and economic problems including VD, wounds from fighting, malnutrition, abortion, alcoholism and the like. The bar girl also comes to the clinic with VD. While in the queue, they hear about and discuss some of the youth brigades that have been started in the area.

Youth brigades at the growth centre are then shown engaged in various economic activities including carpentry, construction of buildings, sewing and so on. The boy and the girl have also joined the brigade. They fall in love and decide to get married. But news arrive that the boy's mother is very sick. The boy goes back to the village and has to stay and take care of the mother and the family. Using the skills learnt from the youth brigades, he starts economic activities in the village. The girl later returns to the village to get married but first she starts economic activities for her family. They get married and have a big wedding.

The skit for this dance drama was first roughly strung together at the workshop centre and then taken to the Murewa shopping centre for rehearsals to allow the members of the community to participate in shaping it. The audience enthusiastically discussed each scene and gave ideas on how to improve it. Especially the youth, very willingly participated in all the roles that involved the youth. It was easy for them to get in and express their own experiences. Most of the major roles were played by the local residents. Local dance groups supplied the dance music and participated in the dancing.

The discussions revealed some interesting class interests. For example, the business men were very vocal on issues concerning the fate of the liquor stores. The political leaders, on the other hand, insisted that the attack on the councillor by the gang of youth was improper. They actually convinced the rest to change the victim of this attack to someone with no political standing. It was interesting that a year after this workshop, a councillor was actually attacked by the unemployed youth at the Murewa growth point. Stephen Chifunyise, a participant in this group comments on this event in the Herald (Zimbabwe) under the heading "Murewa dance drama was real and prophetic":

> The Sunday Mail report of July 15 demonstrate vividly how prophetic the dance drama was about the future of Murewa growth point ... In the dance drama, the unemployed young men form gangs and begin to terrorise the growth point. One of the most significant results of this terror is that a district councillor is beaten and robbed by the gang while on his way from a bottle store late at night ... During the creation of this scene, local political leaders disagreed with the scenario because they believed that it was wrong to show in a play a district councillor being beaten and robbed by unemployed youths. Because of this view, the scene was cut out of the dance drama. It is interesting to note that the Sunday Mail report says that among the numerous victims who have been assaulted at the growth point is the district chairman, Cde J. Gamba ...

In spite of the active participation of the local people in the work-performance, the group could not reach a stage of strategising with the members of the community on the specific action to be taken to resolve the portrayed problems. This was basically because the group never quite managed to establish a base in the community, especially since the growth point was semi-urban with the households living more on an individual basis than would be the case in a village community. On the other hand, this was a general weakness of the whole workshop because even those groups working in the villages did not accomplish the strategising for action. A lot of it had to do with organisational problems arising from the fact that the workshop was too big, involving about a hundred people. The area covered was also too large to monitor effective results. And as Eyoh[1] also observes, the Zimbabwean organisers were too pre-occupied with their own internal differences to pay much attention to the realisation of the goals of the Murewa workshop. Indeed, at the end of it there was a general feeling that a lot was left undone, in spite of the great enthusiasm of the local people. Murewa was one good example of how careful Popular Theatre workers ought to be in terms of who participates as animateurs. The presence of too many bureaucrats, who were not very much interested in the grassroots people but

---

1. Eyoh, H. 1986, *From Hammocks to Bridges*, BET & Co Ltd., Yaounde.

instead wanted to use the workshop as a possible stepping stone to higher posts, proved to be a big stumbling block preventing the Murewa workshop from becoming a success.

Even though Murewa caused quite a stir in the local area while it lasted it does not seem to have had a lasting impact on the use of theatre for development. Consequent work in Zimbabwe has been restricted to the use of theatre to train adult educators and the formation of some theatre groups for the urban workers through the work of ZIMFEP.

For the Popular Theatre movement though, the Murewa workshop's most obvious contribution was the proof that the use of people's own art forms produces the most effective participation from the members of the community. Previous Popular Theatre undertakings in Southern Africa and Nigeria had undermined the place of People's own theatre forms in the Popular Theatre process. There was an apparent push for the use of drama and sometimes even an indication that drama and Popular Theatre were synonymous. There were attempts in Southern Africa to use dance, but dance was only conceived from the point of view of dance drama. Where the traditional dances were performed as they were known by the local people, it was to provide interludes or to keep away the noisy children from the discussions.

Various reasons could be advanced for this state of affairs. One is that most of the people involved in organising the earlier Popular Theatre in Southern Africa and Nigeria were European expatriates, including people like Ross Kidd, Martin Byram, Andrew Horn, David Kerr, Brian Crow, and Michael Etherton. Their European cultural background accounts for the limitation of their theatrical knowledge and skills to only the dramatic genre. As such they saw theatrical undertakings only from the point of view of drama. However, considering that the 1970s represented a very active period for the assertion of African cultural identity, as seen in the many efforts to create an authentic African theatre movement based on the African cultural identity, the insistence of the Popular Theatre workers on the use of drama of the European type calls for other explanations.

It could be taken as one form of neo-colonialism, whereby the expatriates deliberately ignored the indigenous theatre forms because they believed in the superiority of European theatrical forms. Just as they continued to maintain European literature and drama syllabi in the universities where most of them taught and from which they conducted the Popular Theatre workshops, they extended the European drama tradition to the Popular Theatre movement. In a way this could also be taken as their own projection into the future in the sense that with the mounting noise over the irrelevance of European theatre and the increasing demand for theatre to be linked to development, their job future was in Popular Theatre. But for them to be experts in Popular Theatre, the form had to be drama because they could not be experts in African traditional dance or heroic recitation or story-telling.

On the other hand, the disregard for the indigenous theatre forms could be simply a matter of ignorance. Most of these expatriates were either adult education teachers or English literature experts. Their theatrical skills were very limited. The adult education expatriates came upon theatre, or to be precise, role playing as a tool in effecting adult education programmes. Inspired by Paulo Freire's ideas on education and the successes of role playing in Peru and other parts of Latin America, they wanted to try it in Africa. But in a typical expatriate fashion, they imposed role playing in Africa without adapting it to the local theatrical conditions. Their limited theatrical knowledge prevented them from realising that role playing is not limited to drama but can also be achieved through dance or any other theatre form.

In a way, the presence of these expatriates in the organisation of the Murewa workshop contributed towards the non-effective use of the rich and active Zimbabwean traditional theatrical heritage. Much of this local vibrancy was wasted only on warm up exercises or the one big *Pungwe* (an artistic festival), organised one afternoon, not as part of the workshop process but merely to bring the guest artists and the local dance groups together. But Murewa did bring out the fact that in some parts of Africa the indigenous theatre forms still play a very active role in the lives of the people and, therefore, that there is great potential for their use in Popular Theatre. Indeed, if we are talking of a people's culture then their own theatrical forms is the only logical choice for Popular Theatre work.

It is a fact that even though the Europeans tried very hard to establish the European drama tradition, it remains an art form of the elite or the urban populations. There is a dramatic tradition in all African societies but it must not be taken to be synonymous with European drama. There is a need for Popular Theatre workers to seek out those forms, dramatic or other, which are the people's own and then use them as a tool for conscientisation and mobilisation for development.

It is surprising, therefore, that the Kumba workshop held in Cameroon one year after Murewa made little effort to explore the use of the indigenous theatre forms in the Popular Theatre process. A full report of the Kumba workshop is contained in *From Hammocks to Bridges*.[1] As the report shows, the workshop had many successes if compared with Murewa, especially in terms of organisation, controlling the number of participants and reducing the area of operation. One of its major successes cited was in Konye village where it was found that the village was divided into three feuding chieftaincies. The conflicts between the three was so deeply entrenched that they could not come together to solve the problem of constructing a bridge critical to the transportation of their agricultural produce of cocoa and food crops. Through the workshop the three groups came together and raised the money for the construction of the bridge.

In terms of the theatrical process, however, Kumba resorted to the old approach, almost of the *Laedza Batanani* where a group of theatre workers and extension workers, in this case community development students, did most of the theatrical work, thus restricting the participation of the village to discussing the content of the performance. The fact that the workshop team spend a few nights in the villages did not result in as much participation of the villagers in the theatrical process as was expected. It only improved the team's perception of the problems and their rapport with the local people.

An interesting issue arising out of the Kumba workshop which is only briefly raised in its report, is related to the question of the animateur. Who should be the animateur was briefly discussed with reference to the bureaucrats in Murewa. But the question of who should be the animateur and what kind of behaviour is expected of him or her is an issue that has not been seriously dis-

---

1. Eyoh, H. 1986.

cussed in Popular Theatre circles in Africa. After introductory remarks to participants on the importance of properly relating to the local people and the need to enable the members of the community to identify with the members of the Popular Theatre workshop coming from outside the community involved, not much effort has gone into following up how the members of the workshop team fare in their role as animateurs. It is normally taken for granted that they are good animateurs. It is normally taken for granted that they are good animateurs. But sometimes things happen that seriously question the commitment of Popular Theatre participants. The Kumba workshop offered one good example of the contradictions that can be faced in the personal behaviour of the animateur in relation to the objectives of the Popular Theatre cause. What follows is a description of one such incident, which the author, who was a participant in the Kumba workshop, witnessed.

Our group was in Konye village where the fourteen of us were living in several houses with different families. All the female participants, including myself, were living in one house. In spite of reminders, these girls, who were students of a community education college in Kumba town, made little effort to interact with the host family. Not only did they refrain from spending time with the members of the family, they had to be reminded to assist in laying the table and washing the dishes at the end of the meals. Most of their time outside the official workshop timetable was spent at the liquor stores in the company of the workshop team members. The girls also dressed up in a fashion very distinctly different from that of the village. In fact, they went to the extent of changing their clothes twice a day when many of the villagers wore the same clothing for a number of days. Their dress fashions, and the quality of the fabrics, were also distinctly superior to the clothing of the villagers. The time spent on make-up and nail-polishing was very characteristic of city life. This is not to say that Popular Theatre animateurs should not look smart, rather this goes to show how insensitive the girls were to the fact that their behaviour and personal appearance could widen the gap between them and the people they were supposed to work with in order to bring out their problems and analyse them together with a view to solving them.

This attitude was extended to a ritual which the Konye women had prepared especially to welcome the workshop team to the village. Carrying different types of food they had spent the whole day preparing, the women arrived at the house where the girls were staying. The other members of the team plus the men of the village were also there. The women placed the dishes on the table and asked me, as the group's leader, to break the kola nut. After the kola nut ritual we were invited to eat the food. Most of the workshop team members refused to eat saying that they had already eaten. Most of the food, therefore, lay on the table untouched.

Then the women started dancing around the room and the workshop team joined them. After the first dance, however, I realised that I was the only one from the workshop team on the dancing floor. Except for one girl who was sitting down because she was ill, the rest had disappeared. I came to learn the following day that they had all gone to the liquor store to drink, regardless of the fact that the Konye women had actually brought drinks with the food. The dance, however, was scheduled to go on until midnight so I was on the dance floor dancing on behalf of everybody else. It became difficult for me and the women to communicate because I did not know the local language and the workshop participants who knew the language were not there to translate. The women made special arrangements to bring a young man who could speak English. This young man had to be on the dance floor throughout, translating the songs and the conversation between me and the women. The women were obviously offended by the cold shoulder they had received from the workshop team and they told me as much, adding that the city people always looked down on the villagers. I apologised on behalf of the others and tried to assure them that I appreciated their hospitality.

Then at midnight the women prepared to perform the closing ceremony of the ritual. The two sides had to share the last amount of liquor consumed during the ritual. So two small glasses were filled with the last liquor and put on the table ready for the ceremony. As we did with the kola nut, I had to take one glass and a representative of the women the other glass. Just as the ceremony was about to commence, one of the girls from the workshop team walked in with a liquor bottle in her hand. She walked to the table, picked one of the two glasses, threw its content on the floor and walked away to her bedroom, presumably to use the glass to drink the liquor she had brought with her.

There were a few seconds of shocked silence. Then one woman broke into a spontaneous song that was immediately picked up by the other women and a skit was improvised to accompany the song. It was a song of anger at the ill treatment they received from the city women. Unfortunately the song came so suddenly that I could not record it. In fact, since I had to be dancing all the time it was not possible for me to record any of the ritual. There followed a half hour of song, dance and improvisation where the village women vented their anger at the humiliation they had been subjected to. They decided to make Eyoh, the local liaison for the workshop, the target for their improvisations. One of the songs was about Eyoh, who had gone to the city and, ignoring the warning against city women, had brought to Konye village not only one woman, but many city women (the workshop girls). These city women had no respect for the village women and now they had even spoilt their ritual. Another song demanded that Eyoh pay a fine on behalf of his city women.

In the end, Eyoh had to placate the anger of the women by apologising through dance and song and offering a full bottle of liquor as a sign of repentance. This bottle was shared among the women and the last of its liquor used for the closing ceremony.

The worst aspect of this incident was that the members of the workshop team involved in this incident did not seem to be much bothered when the irregularity of their behaviour was pointed out. It did not prevent some of them from talking down to the villagers during meetings in the subsequent workshop processes.

A factor which Popular Theatre cannot ignore is the important role that the Popular Theatre participant can play as animateur. Participation in Popular Theatre is not only a question of having theatre skills. It is a commitment to a process through which a people can be animated to better its conditions. It is crucial for those who participate as organisers and principal participants to be aware that they are involved in a consciousness raising process. Their own consciousness, therefore, needs to be of a level that will facilitate raising the awareness of other people. Personal behaviour may seem trivial but it can spoil the whole process by destroying people's confidence in the process. Identifying with the members of the community one is working with is just as crucial. Here one is not talking of the form of identification that Africa has seen in participatory research where anthropologists have dressed up in animal skins. It is perhaps better to identify with the people in a way that enables them to take the animateur as a person who not only respects them but is genuinely interested in their welfare.

In fact it has been debated whether it is proper for Popular Theatre to operate with an external team going into a community and trying to work with people to solve their problems. This is frequently the case in Africa, where the Popular Theatre workers are often expatriate or middle class theatre artists and university lecturers. It has been argued that the differences in class between these people and people at grassroot level prevents a meaningful realisation of the Popular Theatre goals. However, it should be noted that people from outside or within a community can play an effective role if they understand their role in Popular Theatre as being primarily that of animateur, facilitating critical analysis of issues; ensuring the participation of all interest groups; broadening views where they are too narrow or restricted; facilitating discussion without imposing one person's ideas. The broader world view on intellectuals can positively contribute towards a better analysis of the situation at the grassroot level. But this is only possible if the Popular Theatre participants first grasp their role as animateur. The Popular Theatre movement still has to grapple with this problem.

The Kamiriithu Popular Theatre event in Kenya provided another very significant contribution to the Popular Theatre movement in Africa. In 1977 a number of University of Nairobi lecturers decided to participate in reviving the Kamiriithu Community Education and Cultural Centre (KCECC). The objective was to make the adult education classes, which was the first activity of the centre, a liberating process through which the Kamiriithu peasants' awareness of being exploited could be raised. The University people, who were the animateurs, used the literacy classes and theatre productions to expose the fact that the poverty in Kamiriithu had roots in an unjust economic system where a few members of the society, in alliance with foreign capital are exploiting the majority. As Kidd observes, "the peasants and workers, who had done all the fighting in the forest, lost out. They remained on the whole landless, poor, subject to the same exploitative working conditions and without an effective means of political expression and participation".[1] The aim of the Kamiriithu Popular event was to conscientise the people thus preparing them to better confront the sources of their poverty.

The process started with literacy classes for adults and children who did not go to school. The literacy programme encouraged the participants to question the status quo and to understand the causes of their landlessness and poverty. The participants also became organisers of their own programme by making some decisions on the curriculum, recruiting teachers and mobilising village support. In searching for a medium that would maximise the villagers' participation, the animateurs chose Popular Theatre.

According to Kidd, the Kamiriithu Popular Theatre process involved several meetings by a cultural committee to decide on the content of the play. Ngugi wa Thiong'o and Ngugi wa Mirii were then requested to write a draft playscript reflecting the problems in the village and using the local language, Kikuyu, and other expressions from the people. The play draft was then discussed by the participants, and amendments were made. The play *Ngahika Ndeenda*[2] *(I Will Marry When I Want)* was the result. Collective creation continued during seven weeks of public rehearsals, culminating in public performances that attracted audiences even from outside Kamiriithu.[3]

The success of Kamiriithu was not only due to the quality of its animateurs, but also to its ability to realise the participation of members from all age groups of the community. Traditional Kikuyu dances and songs of struggle were incorporated into the play allowing the peasants to unleash their rich artistic talents in an expression of their suffering. *Ngahika Ndeenda* was the story of their lives, their struggles, concerns and hope. It is the story of Kigunda, a poor farm labourer. His exploitation by Kioi, his employer, is portrayed through the abject poverty in which

---

1. Kidd, R. 1983.
2. Ngugi wa Thiong'o and Ngugi wa Mirii 1982, *I Will Marry When I Want*, Heinemann, London.
3. Ngugi wa Thiong'o 1982.

Kigunda's family lives, and also through the sexual exploitation of his daughter Gathoni, who is impregnated by Kioi's son and then jilted. Kioi also swindles Kigunda out of his small plot of land and enduces him to drinking. The suffering of the worker is at the same time shown through the plight of Gicaamba, a worker at Bora shoe company. At the end of the play, the workers and the peasants call for the mobilisation and unity of the poor to end the land grabbing, abuses, slave working conditions, and their all-round exploitation.

The play production was accompanied by a collective and self-help construction of an open air theatre with a seating capacity of about 2,000. This theatre was, however, razed by the government in 1982, in a clamp-down on the Popular Theatre event that included the closure of the Kamiriithu centre, the detention of one of the organisers, Ngugi wa Thiong'o between 1977 and 1980, and eventually, the flight from Kenya of several animateurs, including the two Ngugis, Gecau Kimani and Micere Mugo. The villagers did sustain enough strength to continue running the centre until it was closed down, despite Ngugi's detention. But the repression after their second production, *Maitu Njugira (Mother Sing for Me)*, forced the village to capitulate.

The coming to a standstill of the Kamiriithu theatre endeavour, quoted as "the most successful use of people's theatre in developing critical consciousness and mobilising people for collective action",[1] brings us to yet another significant issue which Popular Theatre in Africa has yet to resolve. This is the issue of giving Popular Theatre an organisational base that would ensure the long term sustenance of the popular theatre process. The lack of an organisational base, and therefore the limited impact of Popular Theatre in Africa has been pointed out. Assessing *Laedza Batanani*, Kidd comments that:

> In Botswana's Popular Theatre programme, the organisational strategy for moving people to action has been unclear. Most community organisations are weak and only represent elite interests in the community. Organisations with a more popular base need to be developed to provide the leadership for organising both the Popular Theatre programme and follow-up action. At present, the programme is built around the involvement of government extension workers as actors-animateurs. These

---

1. Kidd, R. 1983.

are becoming more committed to progressive social change but they are still influenced by the traditional development issues—concerned with modifying the deficiencies of the poor—and are constrained from getting too deeply involved in sensitive political issues. The organisational base now needs to be broadened.[1]

And Michael Etherton sums up his experiences in Nigeria:

In Africa, there seems to be an absence of any effective organisational framework to provide continuity, apart from the ruling or dominant political parties. Theatre work needs to be keyed into organisations which are concerned with raising consciousness and strengthening people's culture rather than with acquiring and holding on to political power. The drama may well become a key methodology for developing thought across a broad front as a basis for future company, the university drama department are all politically inadequate organisations.[2]

There is a general lack of grassroot organisations in Africa, that is, organisations which are run by the people themselves, and which have the political, economic, and social power to sustain themselves. Popular Theatre has yet to find the most suitable organisational structure to sustain its process. This argument could, however, be turned around, and an argument advanced that Popular Theatre is needed precisely because the grassroots have been denied the power to organise their lives. The success of Popular Theatre should, perhaps, be measured from the point of view of how it can best serve as a tool through which the dominated classes can organise all aspects of their welfare.

Raising another aspect, the Kamiriithu case represents a good example of what Popular Theatre can suffer in the hands of repressive governments. It serves to remind the Popular Theatre advocates that the ruling classes will not always take kindly to the promotion of the peasants' and workers' culture of resistance and struggle. Popular Theatre is essentially a struggle with the dominant forces whose positions are threatened by any possible awakening of a people's awareness or the sharpening of their consciousness. How to operate without causing a head-on collision with the powers bound to wreck the Popular Theatre process is the question left to the African Popular Theatre movement by Kamiriithu.

---

1. Kidd, R. 1979.
2. Etherton, M. 1982, *The Development of African Drama*, Hutchinson, London.

In spite of the shortcomings of the various models pointed out in this section, the Popular Theatre movement in Africa can be taken as a genuine attempt to approach the development of a people from the totality of their way of life. Theatre is here used not only to sharpen their awareness and thus enable them to confront their social and economic realities, but also to involve them as active participants in their own development.

To provide more specific and detailed examples, the rest of the study is devoted to specific practical case studies of Popular Theatre. The case studies are taken from Tanzania for two reasons. One is that the author has participated as animateur in the workshops cited and, therefore, is in a position to supply detailed information on the process involved. Secondly, Tanzania Popular Theatre offers a Popular Theatre model different from what has been happening elsewhere in Africa.

The Tanzanian model offers an interesting contribution to Popular Theatre practice in two major aspects. One is that the members of the community themselves are the participants in all the stages of the Popular Theatre process. Together with the animateurs, who act primarily as catalysts, the members of the community do the research, analyse the issues arising and then become the performers to concretise their situation theatrically after which they strategise on follow-up action. Secondly, the Tanzanian model is based on the community's indigenous popular theatre forms. Indigenous dances, story-telling, mime and dramatic skits are the theatrical forms used. Using such forms ensures the effective participation of the community concerned.

The Tanzanian movement has had the advantage of an existing theatre movement encouraging the promotion of Tanzanian indigenous forms, as discussed in the following chapter. Also, as it will be shown later, it has the advantage of an existing grassroot structure of the *Ujamaa* village where people already live as a unit and mobilise each other for various economic, political and social issues. The *Ujamaa* village structure has a village chairman and a council of twenty-five members. This council, which is elected, organises and mobilises the people into the different village activities through various committees. The rest of the community are often called to public village meetings to discuss the village plans and programmes. Mobilising people for developing action is not out of the ordinary. People are used to getting together, discussing and debating issues in public. Mobilising them to participate in Popular Theatre, therefore, is relatively easy.

The difference with Popular Theatre, though, is that the agenda is formulated by the people themselves as opposed to the normal practice dealing with issues coming from the government or the Party. Also in Popular Theatre, their participation takes a theatrical form instead of the official meetings where the officials tend to dominate and sometimes bulldoze people into decisions. This is not to say that the *Ujamaa* village is the ideal grassroot structure sought by the Popular Theatre movement. But it has in this case provided one example of a structure at the grassroot level that could be of use. Of course the *Ujamaa* village being part of a national structure imposed from above can have its own disadvantages in terms of the people. However, the *Ujamaa* village unit has given the Popular Theatre in Tanzania a convenient structure through which people could be brought together. As will be seen, this structure was particularly useful in providing a forum for follow-up action. For example, because the local theatre groups were a recognised unit in the village set-up, they could carry on to organise more Popular Theatre work in the absence of the animateurs. Also the village structure enabled the people to take follow-up action after the workshops as was the case in the allocation of land to the youth of Malya (see chapter 7) and the sending of the delegation to the regional authorities in Mkambalani (see chapter 10). In a way, the Tanzanian model goes one step further towards facilitating a more meaningful participation by the people.

CHAPTER 6
The theatre in Tanzania

The use of theatre to advance popular interests has a long history in Tanzania. This is obvious in the well documented history of Tanzanian theatre as seen in a number of documents including *Tanzanian Traditional Theatre as a Pedagogical Institution*, (Mlama),[1] *The Development of East African Drama*, (Hussein),[2] *Politics and Theatre in Tanzania after the Arusha Declaration*, (Lihamba),[3] and *The Major Trends in Tanzanian Theatre Practice*, (Mlama).[4] These works show the role that Tanzanian Theatre, both indigenous and foreign, has played in the pursuit of economic, social and political ideas.

Tanzanian Traditional Theatre as a Pedagogical Institution outlines how some of the indigenous theatre forms were woven into the formal and informal educational processes of Tanzanian traditional society. Dance, story-telling, mime and some rituals were effective tools through which specific values and attitudes were imparted on people and the basis of behaviour in the society charted out. The study also outlines the Popular base on which most of this theatre was built. In many societies, the creation of both form and content was constructed on the broad participation of the members of the community, who as performers or audience could use the theatre to express their concerns and viewpoints.

In outlining the historical development of European drama in East Africa, Hussein highlights the emergence of some popular theatre forms that represented popular interests. The *Vichekesho* (comic skits) of the 1970s, after the Arusha Declaration that intro-

---

1. Mlama, P. 1983, *Tanzanian Traditional Theatre as a Pedagogical Institution*, Ph.D. thesis, University of Dar es Salaam.
2. Hussein, E. 1975.
3. Lihamba, Amandina 1986, *Politics and Theatre in Tanzania after the Arusha Declaration*, Ph.D. thesis, University of Leeds.
4. Mlama, Penina,1986, *The Major Trends in Tanzanian Theatre Practice*, paper presented to the Janheinz Jahn Symposium, Mainz.

duced *Ujamaa*, became the theatre of the working class. Through the *Vichekesho*, the Tanzanian workers rallied behind socialism and exposed the capitalist forces responsible for their exploitation and oppression.

Lihamba goes on to show the specific role these *Vichekesho* and other popular forms such as *Ngonjera*, have played within the context of socialist ideology. Although, as mentioned earlier, a lot of the theatre activities patronised by the state toe the Party line, there are some forms that have significantly represented the interests of the Tanzanian common man and woman. The boss of the Parastatal company, who misappropriates public funds, the official who overlooks people's rights, the sufferings of the peasants due to official mismanagement are just some of the concerns of such theatre forms.

The Major Trends in Tanzanian Theatre Practice, on the other hand, shows the complexity of the Tanzanian Theatre scene, reflecting the effects and impact of various historical factors. Tanzanian theatre is not a single body of activities. Rather, it is a variety of movements constantly feeding into and influencing each other. From the pre-capitalist theatre forms, whose form and content depend on the varying ethnic socio-economic structures but was largely utilitarian, Tanzania saw the introduction of the bourgeois European theatre with the British colonialism and its accompanying capitalism. The over-emphasise on entertainment over and above other functions of theatre became a significant feature of this theatre. Although after independence in 1961, the ruling elite strived to promote the indigenous Tanzanian cultural identity through the revival of traditional dances, they largely overlooked the educational and other functions of such forms. They therefore promoted the dances merely for entertainment as was seen in the National dance troupe established in 1962.

1967 is a landmark in the history of Tanzania, not only from an economic or political point of view, but also in that it was the beginning of an era that brought very significant changes to the country's theatre practice. *Ujamaa*, as stipulated in the Arusha Declaration, believes in the absence of exploitation of man by man, the ownership of the major means of production by the peasants and workers, self-reliance and human equality.[1] The adoption of *Ujamaa* has resulted in various major steps being taken to direct the country's development policies and plans towards socialist construction. The nationalisation of the major means of production, the reorganisation of agricultural production through villagisation, the decentralisation of regional and district planning, the reorganisation of industrial management and the adoption of an education for self-reliance policy are some examples. These steps which had a direct bearing on the lives of people were very soon reflected in the theatre.

For example, the enthusiastic reception of the Education for Self-Reliance policy of 1967,[2] which called for a curriculum relevant to the Tanzanian environment and the fostering of socialist values, dealt a blow not only to British history, British geography, English literature but also to the British theatre then dominant in the educational institutions. All of a sudden European plays and indeed, European aesthetics were irrelevant and associated with capitalism and imperialism. Just as many foreign textbooks were taken away from the shelves of school libraries, European theatre abruptly disappeared from the school stages. Since the schools were the main exponents of European theatre this meant almost the total disappearance of the European theatre practice from the Tanzanian theatre scene.

Between 1967 and 1986 there have been only about six productions of European plays by a Tanzanian cast for a Tanzanian audience: *The Trojan Women* (University Theatre Department, 1968), *The Vulture,* an adaptation of Swartz's *The Dragon,* (University Theatre Department, 1968), Nyerere's Swahili translation of Shakespeare's *The Merchant of Venice* (University Theatre Department, 1969), Mushi's Swahili translation of Sophocles' *Oedipus,* (Butimba College of Art, 1983), Chekov's *The Bear,* (University Theatre Department, 1969) and Brecht's *The Measures Taken,* (University Theatre Department, 1976).

In fact most groups have a preference for adaptations and even then the cases are far between. The exclusively expatriate "Little

---

1. Nyerere, Julius 1967, *Ujamaa,* Oxford University Press, Oxford.
2. Nyerere, Julius 1967, *Education for Self-Reliance,* Government Press, Dar es Salaam.

Theatres" in Dar es Salaam and Arusha are exceptions. They stage exclusively European plays and since their formation in 1947 and 1953, respectively, they have continued to cater for the pastime of the European community by staging the off-season productions of West End and Broadway. They have remained oblivious to the local Tanzanian theatre and many Tanzanians, on the other hand, are unaware of the existence of these two theatres while those who are, dismiss them as a non-issue.

Due to the little attention given to European theatre, basically because of the irrelevance of the theatre that was introduced to Tanzania by the British, today the younger generations, unlike their parents, are hardly ever exposed to the European type of theatre, nor to such names as Shakespeare, Molière or Brecht. The furthest theatre groups would go in producing foreign plays is staging plays from other African countries. For example, in its ten years of existence, 1976 to 1986, Paukwa, a leading amateur theatre group has staged only three foreign plays: Soyinka's *The Swampdwellers* 1980, Fugard's *The Island,* and Ruganda's *The Burdens,* both in 1981. There is no European play in their repertory. This goes to show that in Tanzanian contemporary theatre practice, relevance is no longer an issue for debate.

The adoption of socialism also provided a fertile ground for the emergence of new theatre forms. Even the elite who had been significantly alienated from their indigenous theatre and trained to promote only European theatre responded positively to the challenge of coming up with a new theatre that would be relevant to the country's socialist aspirations. Even when using European theatre conventions, they embarked on an attempt to build up a theatre movement that would answer to the demands of the new society. New plays with Tanzanian content were written, improvised and produced. Between 1968 and 1986, 50 plays have been published, all of them in Kiswahili, the national language. Many more have remained unpublished or unscripted.

Analysing the post-1967 plays, Lihamba observes that they responded to the reality after the Arusha Declaration by utilising prevailing attitudes, ideas, moods and expectations of the period to create works which reflected and showed a desire to act on that reality. Most of the earlier plays of this period, she argues, strongly support *Ujamaa* as a viable political and economic mode of organising society. They provide a rationale as to why *Ujamaa* is preferable and how it should function. Hussein's *Mashetani*,[1] Muhando's *Hatia*,[2] Ngahyoma's *Huka*[3] and Mbogo's *Giza Limeingia*[4] are some examples.

Later plays take a more critical view of the Arusha Declaration. Pessimism, disillusionment and protest over the non-delivery of the goods promised by *Ujamaa*, exposure of problems and a call for the eradication of growing contradictions characterise the plays of the second decade of socialist policy. Examples include *Harakati za Ukombozi* (Lihamba et al.),[5] *Kaputula la Marx* (Kezilahabi),[6] *Ayubu* (Paukwa),[7] *Lina Ubani* (Muhando),[8] *Nguzo Mama* (Muhando),[9] *Mafuta* (Paukwa),[10] and *Mnyonge Hana Haki* (Katoke),[11] all of them written and produced after 1977.

The production of these plays has centred mainly around educational institutions and especially the colleges of art in Butimba and Bagamoyo, and the University of Dar es Salaam's department of Art, Music and Theatre. Play productions are also part of the annual Arts Competition by the Ministry of Culture which brings together groups from all over the country. From the point of view of form, a lot of experimentation has gone into the search for a theatre medium that would be both authentically Tanzanian and relevant to contemporary needs. Research into traditional theatre forms and practical experimentations have brought story-telling, dance, recitations and mime techniques into contemporary stage

1. Hussein, E. 1971, *Mashetani*, Oxford University Press, Nairobi.
2. Muhando, P. 1972, *Hatia*, East African Publishing House, Nairobi.
3. Ngahyoma, N. 1975, *Huka*, Tanzania Publishing House, Dar es Salaam.
4. Mbogo, I. 1980, *Giza Limeingia*, Tanzania Publishing House, Dar es Salaam.
5. Lihamba, Amandina et al. 1976, *Harakati za Ukombozi*, Tanzania Publishing House, Dar es Salaam.
6. Kezilahabi, E. 1981, *Kaputula la Marx*, (unpublished).
7. Paukwa Theatre Group 1980, *Ayubu*, Urban Rural Mission Documentation Centre, Kampala.
8. Muhando, P. 1984, *Lina Ubani*, Dar es Salaam University Press, Dar es Salaam.
9. Muhando, P. 1983, *Nguzo Mama*, Dar es Salaam University Press, Dar es Salaam.
10. Paukwa Theatre Group 1986, *Mafuta*, (unpublished), Dar es Salaam.
11. Katoke College of Education 1984, *Mnyonge Hana Haki*, (unpublished), Katoke.

theatre production. *Ayubu, Mafuta* (Paukwa), *Shing'weng'we* (University Theatre Department), *Azota* (Butimba) and *Chakatu* (Bagamoyo) are some examples.

The same is reflected in the writing for the theatre whereby such plays as *Ngao ya Jadi* (Hussein), *Lina Ubani* (Muhando), *Harakati za Ukombozi* (Lihamba et al.) are innovative blendings of a variety of Tanzanian traditional theatre forms. In actual fact, one wonders whether these works should be called "plays" at all. It can be generally said that the Tanzanian theatre artists of this category have managed to establish a definite theatre movement which, although it may borrow conventions from the West or East, is distinctly Tanzanian in both form and content. The relevance of content, plus the use of Kiswahili and theatrical forms familiar to the Tanzanian cultural setting, have contributed towards reducing the theatrical gap between the masses and the elite which developed in the times of colonisation. Although because of material constraints, these groups do not reach all the sectors of the population, people of all walks of life are normally at home with their productions.

The most popular theatre movement after 1967, though, is that based on Tanzanian traditional dance. In the effort to promote theatre relevant to Tanzania in the educational institutions, traditional dance was the rational choice and a convenient replacement of the colonial European theatre. The ability of traditional dance to accommodate new content also suited the need to use art to propagate the socialist ideology. Thirdly, the culturally inherent ability of the schoolchildren to perform traditional dance enabled them to prepare and stage dance performances even without the assistance of experts. In no time, schools all over the country had formed traditional dance troupes which performed not only at school functions but also in national celebrations and festivals. Unlike their parents, children were now learning and performing Tanzanian dances in the schools. The introduction of dance groups in the schools gave legitimacy to the formation of dance troupes all over the country. The mushrooming of dance performances was also, in a way, a reaction against the colonial suppression of traditional theatre forms.

Recognising the potential of the arts as an ideological tool for the construction of socialism, the ruling Party, then TANU, encouraged a policy of using the arts for political propaganda. In 1968, the Party Chairman, Nyerere, requested the artists to "go and propagate the Arusha Declaration and praise [our Tanzanian] culture". *Ngonjera* emerged in response to this call. The late Mathias Mnyampala, a leading poet and exponent of Ngonjera, combined the art of poetry with dramatic recitation to produce a poetic drama that got the name of *Ngonjera*. Today, *Ngonjera* stands second only to traditional dance in popularity.[1]

The use of theatre for political propaganda saw the formation of theatre groups, basically of traditional dance, music and Ngonjera, in state and parastatal institutions, factories and defence forces. In the rural areas, villages have also formed their own theatre groups under the auspices of village governments. The village groups, however, are not permanent. They are assembled whenever there is need for a performance. These groups perform mainly at political functions, such as rallies, state banquets, and Party meetings at all levels. The ideological intention behind the promotion of these groups has led to the development of a theatre for propaganda which, as mentioned above, is an attempt to domesticate the theatre to serve the interests of the ruling ideology. Indeed, this theatre is little more than a spokesman for the official policy, often uncritically repeating statements by leaders. Often dance songs will come up within a week of a pronouncement of a new policy, repeating the content as given by the government or Party and uncritically supporting it and calling upon everybody to do the same. In fact, one can trace the political history of Tanzania, after 1967, through the dance songs because every major policy step has found its way into dance songs.

The positive aspect of this "official theatre" lies in its success in mobilising theatre performances all over the country. Since theatre performances are a component of official functions and since these functions are held regularly, at village, district, regional or national level, the theatre remains active. In fact the main duty of the district and regional cultural officers today is to mobilise theatre groups for the never ending official functions. The artists them-

---

1. Mnyampala, M. 1970.

selves are often complaining that they are required to perform at too many places.[1]

The disadvantage of this theatre is in its superficiality in dealing with the social economic reality of the society. It has stayed too long at the mere propaganda level. Tanzania has therefore ended up with a very strong theatre which is populist rather than popular since it does not represent the common man's reality or the genuine interests of the majority.

In spite of the genuine intentions to build a socialist state, Tanzania has not been spared the socio-economic crisis afflicting the rest of the developing world. An intensified penetration of finance capital, an increased debt burden, the manipulation by the World Bank, the International Monetary Fund and a host of donor agencies are all part of the problems that have increased the impoverishment of the majority. Believing in the promises of *Ujamaa*, the Tanzania common man and woman worked hard and even sacrificed personal interests for a future common good. By the 1980s though, they were subjected to many hardships including the unavailability of essential commodities like salt, sugar or kerosine. Many people were thrown into a disillusion which bred bitterness and at times despair. The bitterness was accentuated by the apparent treachery of the ruling class which, while everybody was toiling for the common good, managed to amass wealth through corruption and unashamed plunder of the little national resources. The Tanzanian peasant and worker generally felt cheated.

The non-violent reaction of the masses to the crisis, and the lack of demonstrations or street fighting against the government, does not suggest a passive acceptance of the situation. Some people may, indeed, look at it as a sign of docility of the result of a brainwashing that has numbed the ability of the people to protest. To a certain degree that could be a viable argument. But it must be noted that the Tanzanians have, in various ways stood up against the forces of their exploitation. At a national level, they have often rallied behind the government on issues where they realised that the enemy was the capitalist and imperialist forces which strangled the efforts to better their conditions. At the local level, they

---

1. Department of Art, Music and Theatre, University of Dar es Salaam 1983, *Report on the Workshop for Training Artists in Basic Theatre Skills*, Dar es Salaam.

waged wars against the local forces of their exploitation. For example, farmers sometimes refused to plant cash crops contesting the governments claim of the need for foreign currency with an argument that the benefits of the foreign currency did not get back to them. Although not often recorded, heated debates take place in Party and government meetings, especially at grassroot level when people voice their grievances against the ruling class.

The protests have also come in artistic forms. Many songs, *ngonjera* and *vichekesho* have been critical of the system as the following dance song performed by Kilakala theatre group in 1983 illustrates:

> Tunalaani sana enyi viongozi wetu
> Mnaoshiriki madhambi nchini mwetu
> Biashara mwaendesha kwa siri tunatambua
> Biashara uchwara wala msiyakatae.
> Mmekabidhiwa madaraka muongoze
> Mnayatumia kwa manufaa binafsi
> Utasikia simu yapigwa maulizo
> Ngano imefika gunia mbili nyumbani
> Kesho kutwa hotelini maandazi
> Twatambua sana kuwa mnayashiriki
> Watu hatupati ngano imeadimika
> Mnastawisha huko mfaidikako
> Hao hao viongozi na walioshika madaraka
> Hao ndiyo chanzo cha hali ngumu ...

Translation:
We curse you leaders who engage in evil deeds in our country.
You are engaging in private business secretly, that we know.
Petty business and do not say, it is not true.
You have been given positions to lead us but you are using that for your own benefits.
You will hear the telephone inquiring, has wheat flour arrived, two sacks at my house. The day after, buns at the hotel.
We know that you engage in this, we do not get the flour because you send it where you benefit.
It is the leaders in power, they are the cause of our economic hardships.

It needs to be pointed out that Tanzania is seeing art works that are more and more critical in recent times as compared to the earlier years of *Ujamaa*. It must also be noted here that the Tanzanian government, unlike many others in the developing countries, has shown a remarkable tolerance of criticism through the arts and public discussions. This may be due to the Party's own policy of self-criticism or the realisation that such criticism has a contribution to make to the general welfare of the people.

The contemporary Popular Theatre movement in Tanzania needs to be understood in this context. Influenced by the Travelling Theatre movement of the 1960s, Tanzania saw her own travelling theatre based at the University of Dar es Salaam. This travelling theatre, however, could not last long after the changes brought about by the Arusha Declaration, as explained earlier. The travelling theatre idea was therefore dropped by 1970. The next ten years saw a concerted effort by the University in search of a theatre movement suited to the realities of the new society. By 1980, the theatre artists at the University realised that even though their research into traditional Tanzanian theatre forms and their experiments in production had created a solid theatre movement there was still a need to direct this movement towards answering the needs of the people at the grassroot level.

There was a dissatisfaction with the populist nature of "official" theatre and little hope that the institutionally based experimental theatre at the University and the cultural colleges would reach an audience wider than that of the urban areas. The adoption of the Popular Theatre approach in 1980, therefore , was an attempt to provide the missing link. Popular Theatre was meant to promote the people's own theatre practice and to use it to advance their own concerns instead of merely parroting the ideas of the ruling class. The people needed to use the theatre which they already possessed to communicate and analyse their developmental problems especially in the face of the economic crisis.

It was with this objective in mind that the theatre artists from the University of Dar es Salaam, the Bagamoyo College of Art and some Cultural personnel took up the role of animateurs and embarked on a number of Popular Theatre workshops in different parts of the country. Of course, they were aware of the Popular Theatre undertakings in Africa and other parts of the world. They were also aware of the shortcomings of the previous Popular Theatre attempts in Africa.They, therefore, drew upon these experiences to come up with an approach which not only sought to improve on previous effort but one suited to the specific needs of the Tanzanian situation.

A detailed description is given in the following chapters of four Popular Theatre workshops conducted in different parts of Tanzania. These are workshops held in Malya (Mwanza region), Bagamoyo (Pwani), Msoga (Pwani) and Mkambalani (Morogoro). As much detail as possible is given with the intention of giving a close picture of what is involved in a Popular Theatre process. The author participated as animateur in all the four workshops. The documentation of the workshops also has the contribution of the other animateurs, namely: Amandina Lihamba (Malya, Bagamoyo, and Mkambalani), Eberhard Chambulikazi (Malya and Msoga), Gonche Materego (Bagamoyo), and John Masanja (Msoga and Mkambalani).

CHAPTER 7

Malya Popular Theatre Project 1982–1983

This project, referred to as "Theatre for Social Development" (TSD), was geared towards integrating theatre into the development process. It was felt that, if people were to participate actively in development, they must first have an awareness of the need for that type of development. TSD saw in Tanzania a problem in communication about development in the form of a one-way information flow of decrees from above. This communication was impersonal and led to the alienation of the people it was supposed to influence. It also implied that the people had no ability to think critically. This invasion from above had also swept aside meaningful roles of traditional elements like the participation of senior citizens in deciding the affairs of their local areas or the traditional fora like the markets which acted like information centres and places for political debate.

The people's theatre forms were used mainly for political propaganda. In terms of democratic participation, this meant that the people had no effective vehicle that could involve them as a body to express their affirmation or negation or critical response to the process of development.

Objectives of the project

The aim of TSD was to try and redress that situation and to initiate a process in which people would slowly reassert their role as subjects rather than objects of development. TSD aimed at making people use theatre as a means through which they could participate in initiating, discussing, analysing and evaluating their own development process. Theatre as a social form, brings together people and provides a forum for exchange of views and information. TSD was to exploit the people's own popular theatre forms, using the traditional dances, mimes, story-telling and so on as the medium through which the people would communicate issues of concern to their well-being. It was hoped that through this process the people's consciousness would be aroused to come to grips with the problems of development and to move to action to solve them.

Three villages were originally chosen, one each from the coast, Dar es Salaam and Bukoba regions. The reasons for this selection were both practical and artistic. Three villages could be well monitored in the two years of the project without overstretching the capacity of the animateurs. But the three villages also represented three distant cultural zones that would give the Popular Theatre undertaking different experiences of what was possible with the different theatrical forms existing in these areas. Due to financial constraints, however, the three regions were only dealt with in the first phase of familiarisation and study of the socio-economic background. Eventually TSD was only carried out in all stages in Malya village in Mwanza. A team of three animateurs, Amandina Lihamba, Eberhard Chambulikazi, and the author worked on TSD.[1]

The background of Malya village

Malya is a village some seventy-five kilometres from Mwanza town in Northern Tanzania. It is an agricultural village with a population then of about one thousand five hundred. The major agricultural products are rice, maize and cotton. Farming is basically subsistence. A considerable number of livestock is also raised in the area.

Malya is also a small trading centre because it is located at the crossroads for transport to other villages and the town. A considerable number of its inhabitants depend on petty trade for their living. There are also more beer halls than a village of its size

---

1. For further information on this project see the following: Department of Art, Music, and Theatre 1982, *Report on the Malya Theatre for Social Development*, (unpublished); Mlama Penina 1984, "Theatre for Social Development: The Malya Project in Tanzania—Third World Popular Theatre", *Newsletter, International Popular Theatre Alliance*, Toronto.

would normally have in the country. Malya also hosts several government institutions including an agricultural research centre, a folk college and a small scale agricultural equipment factory. The Malya people are originally Wasukuma and they form the majority of the residents.

Research and problem analysis

The team of three arrived in Malya on May the 23rd, after reporting at the Regional and District headquarters as is the government procedure for visiting villages on official business. The team was treated to a big welcome by the village which included meeting the village artists, a communal dinner and dancing. On the following day, the village arranged to stage a play they had themselves prepared for the workshop. A theatre group had been formed one month before in response to the team's first visit. The group brought together artists who had been performing in the village before and this was meant to be the Village Core Group (VCG) for the TSD project.

The play, which was staged before a big audience of the villagers, was about parents who were very strict in the upbringing of their daughter. They locked her up and did not allow anyone to visit her during their absence. When they had to leave her alone in the house, they swept the compound clean so as to be able to detect the footmarks of whoever visited in their absence. In the end, however, the girl gets pregnant. But because she is so scared of what her parents will do, she commits suicide. The man responsible is apprehended, charged with murder and sentenced to death.

In between the scenes and also at the beginning and at the end of the play songs were performed by the village primary school choir. The following is one of the songs:

> CCM ni mapinduzi na sisi tupinduke
> Tusiwe na kasumba za kikoloni
> Nchini Tanzania tunayo kazi kujenga taifa
> Wote Watanzania tufanye kazi kwani kazi ni uhai
> Ujenzi wa Tanzania unategemea Watanzania
> Uchumi wetu Tanzania unakitegemea kilimo
> Tufanye kazi kwa juhudi, tafanye kazi kwa bidii.

Tena wazalendo tuwe macho kuwafichua adui zetu
Wavivu na wazembe pia wote wanaohujumu mali ya umma
Hongera Mwalimu na viongozi wote wa Chama cha CCM
Ni miaka mitano CCM yashika hatamu tutaendelea

Translation:
CCM is revolutionary so we must also be revolutionary
We must not carry on the colonial hangovers
Here in Tanzania we have a duty to build our nation
All Tanzanians must work hard because work is life
The construction of Tanzania depends on the Tanzanians
Our economy depends on agriculture
Let us work conscientiously
Let us work hard
And we patriots must be alert for enemies
The lazy, the fools and those who sabotage our national resources
Congratulations Mwalimu (President Nyerere) and all Party leaders
It is now five years (since the formation of CCM) and CCM is still holding the reigns and we shall advance.

The animateurs decided to take advantage of this gathering to go ahead with the information-gathering stage of the workshop, especially considering that the first two days had already been taken up by the village's own programme. The enthusiasm of the villagers for the programme on the first two days was also a natural introduction to the research stage of the workshop. Immediately after the performance, therefore, the audience was divided into three discussion groups with the assistance of the village organisation committee which was formed a month earlier to be in charge of the workshop. One animateur worked with each discussion group and a discussion was conducted centering around the following questions:

(a) What is your response to the performance?
(b) Does the problem in the play i.e. pregnancy among unmarried girls exist in Malya?
(c) What are the causes of the problem?
(d) What are the possible solutions to the problem?

The response to the performance by all groups was that it was very good entertainment with a lot of truth in it. As to whether the problem existed in Malya, it was unanimously agreed that pregnancy among unmarried girls was a very big problem in the village. Almost three quarters of primary school leavers get pregnant within one year of leaving school. It was also mentioned that there was a widespread habit of uncontrolled use of contraceptives among schoolgirls. The contraceptives were illegally obtained from the dispensary's family-planning unit. There was also an abortion practice carried out by private dispensaries. The problem had grown bigger with time and with the increased dependency on cash income. The causes of the problem were listed as follows:

(a) The need for money as a means to get necessities and also luxury items and the girl's use of their bodies to obtain the money.
(b) Traditional patterns which have encouraged boys to be economically independent and the girls to be dependent on men and the men using that and their money to lure girls.
(c) The girls are not employed and mostly engage in non-income generating activities. In that situation some resort to selling their bodies.
(d) The upbringing is faulty. One view was that parents do their best to bring up their children properly but the girls are corrupted by the environment in which they live. Another view was that some parents encourage their daughters to misbehave, especially the single mother-parents because they cannot cope with the economic situation.
(e) There is a serious breakdown of traditional marriage customs and social patterns of interaction.
(f) Male chauvinism makes the men feel that they have a right to use the girls sexually.
(g) The girls themselves have no self-respect and are not mentally and economically liberated.
(h) Poverty sometimes forces girls to seek money from men and the same makes some parents turn a blind eye to their children's behaviour.
(i) The inflation and unavailability of essential items make those men who have access to such goods use the goods as bait for luring the girls.

(j) The co-education system where boys and girls mix freely encourages them to court each other.
(k) The presence of modern but unsupervised places of social interaction, especially the disco, bars and restaurants give a chance for young people to misbehave.
(l) The problems of poverty, unemployment, inflation or upbringing did not only affect girls. They affected the boys as well. It is only unfortunate that the girls are physically affected by getting pregnant.

Suggestions for solutions included the following:

(a) Practical solutions should be looked into. Suicide is not a solution and in fact it had never happened in Malya.
(b) There is a need to raise the standard of living for everybody. Girls will not be lured by money if they have enough themselves. There is a need, therefore to create employment and meaningful economic activities for primary school leavers.
(c) People have to go back to traditional values of child upbringing and social interaction between the sexes.
(d) The whole village needs to co-operate in the up-bringing of the children in the village. The parents' association WAZAZI should form a disciplinary committee for both parents and children.
(e) Girls should learn to be more self-respecting.
(f) Men should be politicised to respect girls and girls be politicised to be economically independent.
(g) The village should formulate laws to punish both the culprits and the negligent parents.
(h) The national government should also consider assigning local people to fill government posts at the village level, such as the primary school teachers, medical and legal officers. The officers who were not from the local area tended not to take responsibility over their sexual action because they knew that eventually they would be transferred to other areas. Also they had little respect for the local codes of conduct. As such they got the girls pregnant and went away without taking responsibility.

The following day was spent doing more research by talking to different people and moving with the members of the core group to different parts of the village. There were many problems that were brought up including theft of crops in the farms, laziness among some villagers both youth and adults, bang-smoking (a habit that was becoming rampant among the youth), land shortage because large areas of land had been allocated to government institutions in the village. It was agreed that this phase of the workshop concentrate on the issue of youth. Another day was spent on further analysis of the issues that were brought up both at the performance discussion and at the research in the village. This analysis was done by the members of the village core group (VCG) numbering about thirty. Other members of the village also joined the discussion at will and contributed their ideas.

The theatre process

It was decided that the performance by the VCG would form the basis of the workshop theatre production. But that the group would work together to improve on the performance in terms of the content, form and performance skill. The following ten days were, therefore spent on theatre production work.

On the first day there were slightly over one hundred people in attendance including men and women of all age groups. Everybody was free to participate and efforts were made to allow everybody to contribute to the process. Warm-up exercises were done to the local Sukuma dance rhythms. The Wigashe dance was performed by everybody. Other dances were also performed led by the village artists. The animateurs also offered a dance from the Southern part of Tanzania, Kiduo.

The dances were followed by improvisation exercises whereby the participants exercised concentration, moods and expressions under the leadership of the animateurs. Then the participants were requested to think of how the production by the VCG could be reworked to accommodate the discussions and analysis of the Malya situation of the last three days.

On the second day before meeting the participants, the team drew up a draft outline of the play based on the VCG's performance but incorporating the views of the village and their analysis of the situation. At the workshop the participants were asked if anyone had ideas on the production. A few ideas were presented on how to improve the VCG's performance. The animateurs presented their draft for discussion. The draft was discussed and some changes made to it. It was then decided that the draft would form the basis for further collective creation of the production. The production was to combine the various theatrical forms existing in Malya, especially dance and story-telling.

Day three started with warm-up exercises which included the Wigashe dance and two stories narrated by the local participants. One of the stories was about the cruel stepmother who is ill-treating her stepdaughter during the absence of the husband. Eventually she buries the stepdaughter in a pit. A bird then sends the girl's message to her father to come and rescue her from death. The father arrives in time to save her and the stepmother is punished. Choir songs were also performed followed by a traditional Sukuma solo by an elderly woman of about seventy years.

The first scene of the production was then rehearsed. The scene was a festival at the village. People are gathered and a variety of activities are taking place including dances, songs, poetry, and political speeches. During the festival various village characters are introduced. There is Zakia, a schoolgirl from a poor family and Josephine her friend, a girlfriend of a rich businessman who supplies her with a lot of material things. The businessman throws his weight around. He is a playboy and even though he is Josephine's boyfriend, he courts Zakia. Josephine shares her gifts from the businessman with Zakia whom she gives a piece of soap. At the festival are also a group of unemployed boys roaming the streets and doing petty business including selling cigarettes. There is also a group of unemployed girls roaming the streets. They have close relations with the group of boys.

Five boys and five girls acted the two gangs and rehearsed their scenes getting suggestions from the rest on how best to portray the youths. Suggestions included the need to make the boys' petty business more discreet because it was illegal and that the girls be more forthcoming and seeking out the boys. The rest of the participants were split into three groups to separately rehearse the dances and songs they wanted to be part of the festival. The three groups first rehearsed separately and then put their dances together. The roles of Zakia, Josephine, and Madanganya, the businessman, were also assigned and rehearsed.

At the end of the session all the participants were requested to think of a song for particular occasions such as death, courting, farming and so on to be taught to the rest of the participants the next day.

On the fourth day, the participants continued rehearsing the other scenes of the performance after a warm-up with more local dances including the Sukuma dance Bugobogobo, famous all over Tanzania. By now, there was so much enthusiasm for the workshop that the swelling numbers of the participants was proving difficult to control. There was a need to devise ways of controlling especially the children in a way that would allow them to participate without disrupting the rehearsals and especially the on-going discussions on the performance. People were assigned to control the noise in different areas of the performing area but without hindering people from contributing to the creative process.

Scenes two and three were worked out. In scene two Zakia comes home late. There is a quarrel between her and her parents who are displeased with her late return. The poverty of the family is shown especially at the joy of getting the soap which Zakia lies about, saying it is from her school-project. In scene three, Josephine persuades Zakia to go to the disco where Josephine has an appointment with Madanganya. The group of unemployed boys and girls are also at the disco. At the disco Madanganya makes a pass at Zakia but Zakia refuses. Meanwhile Josephine and another girl fight over Madanganya.

The two scenes which were first worked out separately were then run together and the other participants asked to comment. In the discussion it was suggested that in scene two, the parents should not use the soap brought by their daughter without checking where she got it. It was decided that the parents should check with the school instead of settling for flimsy explanations. For scene two, the girls were advised to overcome their shyness. One elder reminded them that they were simply acting the characters and so they should not feel ashamed of the things they were doing to portray the character of loose girls because after all everybody knows that they are only acting. At this session the play was also given the title "Mtoto umleavyo", from a proverb meaning how you raise a child is how he turns out to be.

There had been problems of late arrivals at rehearsals, and therefore the village organising committee reminded everybody to come to the workshop on the assigned times. It was, however, pointed out that those who were employed did not have enough time to walk home, eat lunch and be at the workshop at 3.00, the workshop starting time. Offices close at 2.30 pm. It was decided to push the starting time to 3.30 pm.

The following five days were spent to create the rest of the production. The rest of the storyline included scene four where the businessman is determined to get Zakia. He gives her presents and Zakia agrees to meet him. Zakia takes the presents home and sneaks out to go and meet the businessman. She returns to find that her mother has discovered the gifts. Zakia lies that the gifts belong to Josephine. Josephine comes to say hallo to Zakia but is reprimanded by Zakia's parents for corrupting Zakia. Then Josephine discovers that Zakia has taken away her boyfriend so when the parents leave the two starts fighting. The unemployed boys come to pacify them and offer to sell the gifts at the black market. In the next scene it is discovered that Zakia is pregnant but the businessman refuses to take responsibility. Josephine is also pregnant but is subjected to the same treatment by the businessman. Zakia's parents take Madanganya to court but he gets away with a very light sentence because he bribes the judge. The parents are infuriated and decide to seek justice at the village council.

The play was ended here because this became the entry point for the post-performance discussion with the audience on the issues raised.

Post-performance discussion with the audience

In attendance at the final performance were some six hundred people who received the performance very enthusiastically. Immediately after the performance there was a discussion centering on how the Malya village would solve the problem in the play brought before the village council. The audience was asked to relate their suggestions to the specifics of the realities in Malya. The discussion was chaired by one of the elders who was actively participating in the workshop. The following are the points raised in the discussion:

(a) The youth are not meaningfully engaged, and something ought to be done to solve that problem.
(b) Projects should be started through the rural development bank loans.
(c) Since the youth themselves are not interested in work the village should take the responsibility of starting something for them and persuading them to participate after which they will realise the advantages.
(d) There was a youth project already in the village but the youth did not seem interested. The youth countered this by saying that they are interested in the soap-making project referred to but they had problems of financial and organisational nature that had led to the collapse of the project. The suggestion to form youth projects was, therefore, false unless these problems of the first project were solved.
(e) What was referred to as a youth project was actually not a youth project. It was run by the village government. If the youth were given the chance to run the project themselves things could have been different. So special youth projects need to be started.
(f) Can a youth who is already a failure be trusted to work in a project and succeed? What can the parents or the village do to rehabilitate the youth?
(g) Has the village done anything towards organising the youth and trying to organise the youth from the youth's own point of view?
(h) The problem of child upbringing is very big, especially in connection with young people. The village ought to have a system of guiding and controlling the behaviour of this group. For example, in traditional society the age-set system was used quite effectively. Such systems from among the Wasukuma could be used to bring up the present day youth.
(i) The village should strengthen the security system to check youth behaviour. The committee on security should look into the issue.

(j) When the village plans their overall projects, they should consider projects for the young people and the village should take up the responsibility of guiding them and organising them instead of leaving them to their own devices.
(k) To a large extent both the parents and the village government are at fault for misbehaviour of the youth. There is not much effort to control their behaviour. For example, the youth flock to the disco without any control.
(l) There should be co-operation between the village government and the parents in child upbringing. For example, neither the village government nor the parents do seem bothered about the gang of youth that spends all their time at a jobless corner near Mkulima bar.
(m) The village committee on social welfare is not strong enough to control the youth. By-laws should be set up by the village guard against misbehaviour of both children and parents.
(n) The responsibility of child upbringing should not be left to the individual parents alone but instead be the responsibility of all adults in the village as it used to be in traditional society.
(o) The performance was considered very educational and challenges the villagers to think seriously about the problems of the youth in Malya and how to solve them.

Follow-up action

At the end of the discussion session, it was unanimously agreed that the village should take action to try and resolve the problem of the youth which was the underlying factor behind not only unwanted pregnancies but also a host of other problems. It was agreed that the VCG would sit together with the village council to work out the suggestion of providing meaningful income generating activities for the youth. The village council also promised that from then on, they would try to incorporate the youth question in the development planning of the village.

The workshop continued for another day in order to start up a new production which the VCG was going to continue working on in the absence of the team of animateurs. The other problems existing in Malya which were brought up during the research stage were tabled and the VCG discussed which problem they would deal with. They chose the problem of the unwillingness to work on the land among the young people leading to low food production. A group of six volunteered to work on a draft of a story for the production. The six included two women, two male primary school teachers, one youth and an elder. A discussion was held on the topic to give the six ideas on which to base their draft. It was pointed out that there were two types of such people—youth who were born and raised in Malya and who depended on their parents for their living and those who flocked to Malya from other villages thinking that they could get employment in the government institutions or make a living out of petty business. The reasons as to why they do not engage in agricultural work were given as:

(a) The failure of primary school education to prepare the children for village life as stipulated in the "Education for self-reliance" policy.
(b) That the school leavers still have a preference for wage employment over agricultural work.
(c) That the parents also expect their children to get wage employment after primary school.
(d) Some parents do not set an example to their children because they themselves do not work on the land and they depend on petty business for a living. The increasing blackmarketeering has not helped the situation because now petty business can be lucrative.

The group of six presented the draft to the group on the following day. The outline was that a thief (a young man) is pursued by a crowd. He is caught and beaten. One man who knows him comes to the scene and stops the people from beating him. This man then starts telling the story of the thief. The story is narrated in a storytelling form while the scenes are mimed. The scenes include his failure in school because of inadequacies in the school-system, his seeking employment in the village and failing, starting a small farm but failing, starting petty business and failing too, joining various gangs of bang smokers, disco dancers and resorting to stealing which brings him to the beating by the crowd.

A discussion of the draft produced the following comments from the participants:

(a) The outline should include the reasons why the young man seeks employment e.g. what it is that attracts him to wage employment.
(b) There should be several thieves to portray the fact that there are many people who do not produce. The thieves should be from both Malya and the surrounding villages.
(c) The problem that many people consume but do not produce is not adequately dealt with. The thieves should steal crops from the farms and the crowd pursuing them should be the farm owners. It should be a group of thieves stealing and when people come they all run away except one who is apprehended.
(d) It should be shown that those who consume but do not produce are both the youth and adults.
(e) It should be shown that the kind of family the young man comes from also does not like farming or it encourages him to seek wage employment.
(f) The attempt to start a farm should be at the end as the solution to the problem rather than being part of the problem.
(g) The two groups of producers and non-producers should be shown e.g. there should be a group of farmers who do not sell crops to the state. Instead, the non-producers come to buy from them and then raise the prices.
(h) If the farm fails it should be due to the non-use of proper agricultural methods.
(i) Part of the young man's failure is due to his spending most of the money he earns from petty business on luxuries.
(j) That the youths who are successful in terms of passing their exams and getting employment should also be portrayed.
(k) That the flashback technique was not necessary. Showing the young man as thief first and then showing him as a child in school would bring confusion to the understanding of the play. (Here there was a long discussion on what the storyline could be to replace the flashback).
(l) The story-teller's narration should be based on the defence of the young man's position.

The group of six was requested to rework the draft incorporating the comments of the other participants and to consider using both the flashback and non-flashback techniques. The VCG would then draw up their own programme of work to continue the work on the production. The team of animateurs then left Malya to go back to Dar es Salaam.

The animateur team's third visit

The animateur team made a third visit to Malya three months later, in September 1982. The aim of this visit was twofold. First, the team wanted to find out how far the VCG had managed to continue on their own and to get feedback on the Popular Theatre activities in the past three months. Secondly, the team was to spend some two weeks working with the VCG, taking off from wherever they had reached. The team arrived on September 18th but work could not start for three days because the village was involved in Party elections that were taking place all over the country.

On day four, a meeting was convened between the team and the VCG. The activities of the past three months were reported by the Chairman of the VCG. The group had successfully performed the production on the reluctance to work on the land. In fact Chambulikazi, one of the animateurs, chanced to see this performance when he briefly visited Malya to see the group while on a private visit to Mwanza.

The VCG had also done another production titled *Yaani Yaani* (Blah! Blah!) which took its theme from the Party elections. It exposed the Party leaders who made promises when they sought votes from the people but turned against them after getting into office. *Yaani Yaani* was the name of the character who played the role of the Party leader, full of words but acting contrary to Party leadership by engaging in corrupt practices and abandoning the interests of his constituency. The production was telling people that during the coming elections (which were held during our visit) the Malya villagers should beware of such characters.

Both performances were reported to have received very enthusiastic response from the village. The group attempted to have a discussion after both performances. For the first performance it was agreed that the steps the village council was taking would contribute towards solving the problem of the youth who did not work on the land. This included allocating land to the youth. The youth had argued that they were being accused of not working on the land but actually had no land of their own. The farms belonged to their parents, and even when they worked very hard it was the father who decided how the products of the farm were used, and sometimes the young people did not get a fair return for their effort. So they looked for other things to do to get their own income. The youth were therefore allocated a quarter of an acre each to grow food or cash crops and they were waiting for the farming season to work on their land. The land allocated to the youth had been taken away from the Culture institute which had been given a large piece of land laying unused for five years because the Ministry of Culture had not managed to complete the buildings for the proposed institute.

For the *Yaani Yaani* performances the report was that it did not involve a discussion. This could be explained by the nature of the content in that it was talking of a forthcoming event rather than immediate problems that needed to be resolved.

After the *Yaani Yaani* production the VCG was confronted with problems connected with the group's theatre activities. The problems were that of leadership and interference from the religious leader of the African Inland Church (AIC) in the village. On the question of leadership there was laxity within the leadership of the VCG. When organisational problems arose, the leadership did not discuss them with the members of the group. Nor were they strong enough to solve problems on their own. The chairman and the secretary of the VCG tendered their resignations from leadership to the chairman of the village without discussing the reasons with the group. Therefore the village chairman could not accept their resignations. The chairman and the secretary of the VCG, on the other hand, argued that they did not get the right guidance from the village government. For example, when they tendered their resignation, the village government did not take immediate action to resolve the problems, but only rejecting their resignations. The village committee on culture and social affairs was not informed of the problems and therefore did not take any action.

On the interference from the AIC priest, it was reported that he had reacted negatively to the activities of the VCG claiming that they were contrary to Christian conduct. The priest publicly denounced the activities of the group in his church and threatened his followers with excommunication if they continued participating. The chairman of the VCG, himself a member of this church, was forced to resign due to pressure from the church. It was also reported that some parents of this church rallied behind the priest because of blind faith but also because they had reservations about the personal behaviour of the leaders of the VCG in relation to sex. Both the chairman and the secretary had been responsible for several unwanted pregnancies in the village. The parents therefore felt that their children, especially the girls, would be corrupted.

It was decided that a meeting should be convened in order to resolve the problems. The meeting brought together the village government, the VCG leadership, representatives of the other members of the VCG, and the team of animateurs. The District cultural officer and the Divisional and Branch Party secretariat also attended. The chairman of the village government introduced the purpose of the meeting as the strengthening of the theatre group that had weakened after a spirited beginning. The problems were again presented by the chairman of the VCG, and the accusation that the village government did not take appropriate steps was repeated. The village chairman, however, reported on what the village government had done. The resignation had been refused because it was a matter to be discussed and decided upon the VCG itself before coming to the village government. The matter was discussed at the branch, ward and division level.

The village government then called the AIC priest Yakobo Zebedayo, and discussed the other issues with him. The priest, however, maintained that the VCG's activities were evil. The village government advised the VCG leadership to continue to which the VCG agreed, but later took no action. Then the village government took the initiative to call another meeting of the VCG but the leadership refused to turn up. The Division Party office then decided to form a committee to look into the matter but the committee had not yet started working.

The District cultural officer jumped in at this point saying that in actual fact the existence of the Malya Theatre group was not known and that it had not been registered at his office as the law required. He was, however, corrected. Before the project started the team of animateurs had reported officially to the Regional and District offices, where papers were signed explaining the purpose of the project. If the cultural officer was not aware of this group then it was due to his own office's inefficiency. It was also pointed out that the issue under discussion was how to strengthen the activities of the group and not to bring up bureaucratic issues that could hamper the efforts of the group even further.

It was also reported that there were rumours in the village that the VCG leadership was squandering the VCG funds generated from performances done in Ngudu town in order to have some funds for the group. The VCG chairman countered that the group had a treasurer and a bank account which the members could check.

The meeting resolved that the VCG continues until the existing problems with the AIC had been solved, and that if they wanted to resign this should be an issue for the VCG to decide upon. In order to resolve the religious issue, it was decided that another meeting be convened the next day involving all the religious leaders of all the Christian denominations, Islam and the traditional religions.

On day six the leaders of Islam, the Lutheran, AIC, Anglican, Seventh Day Adventist Christian churches, and the Bagika religion were present at the meeting. Also present were those at the previous day's meeting. The District cultural officer opened the meeting by underscoring the role of culture in development and the relation of religion to man. A question was then put to the religious leaders by the village chairman on what problems the VCG activities posed in relation to their religions. Each of the religious leaders was requested to answer the question on behalf of their faith.

The AIC priest spoke first and said it was difficult for him to speak on behalf of his church. But in his opinion, the failure of the VCG was not due to the AIC because the group is not controlled by that church, and moreover, the group draws its membership from a community wider than that of the AIC congregation. Every individual had the freedom to act according to his faith. He felt that certain cultural activities were good, such as singing in the church or dancing at weddings. This was followed by a call from the floor that the religious leaders should be more frank and specific.

The Islamic leader was of the view that only the action in real life and not the imitation of that action can be evil. Therefore there was nothing wrong with what the theatre group was doing. The Assemblies of God's leadership had nothing against the group except that the priest asked for a change in the timetable of their rehearsals because it interfered with the church's youth activities on Saturdays and Sundays.

The Anglican leader said that some elements in some theatre performances could be unchristian, such as vulgar dancing. But since he had not seen any of the group's performances because he had been away he could not say categorically whether they conflicted with his religion. Then The Seventh Day Adventist Church priest said he had seen and participated in the activities of the VCG and that many members of his church were members of the group. After hearing the rumours that the VCG was questionable, members of his church met to discuss the issue and decided the VCG activities were educational and that members of the church should continue to participate. The Lutheran leader expressed the view that participants should be able to use their faith to guide them in what to do and what not to do. He also said that he did not condone vulgar performances.

The AIC priest spoke again to the effect that the AIC was offended because parents of some participants had complained to the church about the inclusion of such scenes in the play as courting, and the girl getting pregnant. These scenes, they felt, were not only corruptive but also sinful. Secondly, they had claimed that the leaders of the VCG were not of good behaviour and could corrupt their children. He also wanted the VCG to leave Sunday free for religious activities.

After this members of the VCG explained the storyline of their performance to inform those people in the meeting who had not seen the shows.

Then the Anglican leader spoke saying that it seemed the rumours and reactions against the VCG had been started by church leaders who had not seen the performances. After the explanation it was evident that there was nothing wrong with the activities of the group. The leader of the Bagika, a traditional Sukuma religion, also expressed the view that there was nothing wrong with the VCG activities. He added, however, that it was difficult to maintain an artistic group without economic support, according to his experience.

The reactions of the religious leaders were followed by comments by others at the meeting and a general discussion that led to the following resolutions:

(a) The group should continue because there was general agreement that there was no contradiction between its work and religion. It was also resolved that Malya was proud of this group and wanted it to continue.

(b) The leadership of the VCG should continue and be ready to face and solve the problems when they arose. They should also think of how to win the confidence of the parents who do not trust them because of their behaviour.

(c) The village government pledged to strengthen its support for the group and so did the District cultural office.

(d) The VCG was called upon to resume its activities with immediate effect.

In the afternoon of the same day the VCG met and was given a report of all the previous meetings. It was agreed that they would meet the next day and start their activities first with a repeat performance of *Yaani Yaani* merely for entertainment after which they would discuss their next step. The team of animateurs had to leave for Dar es Salaam before the commencement of the group's work but were satisfied that the crisis had been resolved.

The animateur team's fourth visit

The team's fourth visit in January 1985 started with the activity of visiting the farms belonging to the young people, the ones which they had been given as a result of the previous workshops. The young people had responded positively to the farms and had worked on them planting different crops such as maize, groundnuts and cotton. The VCG had plans for a large collective farm for the next season besides these individual farms. A larger farm could also be worked to produce more and increase the income of the members.

The team was also taken to another youth project, a kiosk at the Malya village square serving both as a market and a bus station. The kiosk made of wooden planks and corrugated iron sheets was built on a self-help basis. The village government had donated both the wood and the corrugated iron sheets. Currently, the kiosk was rented by one member of the VCG who paid 150 Tanzanian shillings a month to the group. The long-term plan was to buy utensils and furniture and then employ one of the members of the VCG to run the kiosk under the auspices of the group itself.

There was a new leadership in the VCG because even though the previous chairman and secretary did not resign they did not take action to strengthen the group. Instead, the other members chose new leaders and did a new production on the issue of health facilities in the village. The storyline was of a family with two children both of whom fall sick. The father tries to cure the children with the help of quack doctors *(wapiga ramli)*, but fails and so he goes to the dispensary where one child gets cured but not the other. The family then takes this child to a herbalist who cures the child at a low cost. The draft of this play was an idea of the village chairman, Mzee Ernest Masanja, who had become an enthusiastic participant and tried to keep the group going.

On day two the VCG put on their production on health for the team. After the show the team conducted a theatre skills workshop as a starting point for the work of the following few days. Then it was decided to continue working on the health production. Because the following day was a national festival to mark the Zanzibar Revolution, the group decided to perform their health play at the political rally scheduled for the afternoon at the village square. The whole day was spent working on this production. A discussion was first conducted on the issues around health services in the village. Questions included why the children were not cured by the quack doctor, and why one child was not cured at the modern dispensary. Issues were raised concerning shortage of drugs, incompetence of medical personnel, the selling of drugs from the dispensary to the black market, and general poor health facilities. As to the choice of going to the herbalist it was pointed out that the other alternative would be to go to a far-away hospital, but many villagers could not afford the transport costs. It was felt that it was true that some herbalists could genuinely treat some diseases. It was important to realise that modern and traditional doctors do complement each other.

The production was rehearsed to incorporate these issue. The scene on the doctor and the herbalist was changed to portray the problems of transport in the village and the lack of money to pay the village businessmen who have cars but demand exorbitant fees. One actor refused to perform because he was afraid of the consequences of offending the traditional healers with the portrayal which indicated that some of them are liars. Time was devoted to explaining to him the objectives of the theatre in terms of dealing with the corruptive and anti-social elements. In the end he agreed to participate.

On day three the production was presented at the political rally and was very well received. It was not possible, however, to hold a discussion at the end of it because of the long political agenda of speeches by political leaders from outside Malya. The next four days were spent working on another production, this time centering on the problem of thieves who were stealing ripe crops from the farms at night. This year there was a wave of such stealing whereby thieves literally harvested entire farms and took away all the crops to sell on the black market. People lost the product of a whole season's work as well as a whole year's food supply. More workshops were also added to the programme to try and improve further the theatre skills of the VCG. Emphasis was put on the possibilities which lay in using the local dances for which there were many skills readily available in the village. The team then returned to Dar es Salaam leaving the VCG to continue working on their production.

The animateur team's fifth visit

The next visit to Malya by the team was not possible until five months later and then only one member, the author, could go. At this time Tanzania was facing acute transport problems because of lack of diesel and spare parts. The public transport system had almost come to a standstill. The animateur therefore took three days to arrive in Malya instead of the normal one. At this time a group of ten Oxfam employees from England were visiting Malya as part of their tour to see various Oxfam funded projects in the country. TSD received funding from Oxfam to cover the travelling expenses of the three animateurs so it was included in the Oxfam itinerary.

The team member found the VCG rehearsing two productions, *Walanguzi* (Racketeers) and *Mbio za sakafuni* (Unplanned races end in vain). These had been worked on in the past five months. Since the VCG had already prepared a programme for the special visit of the Oxfam team the animateur decided to just watch the performances and work with the group after the official visit.

On the 5th of June hundreds of villagers together with the Oxfam visitors, who had been accorded a big welcome with dancing the previous day, gathered at the cultural institute hall for the performance. It was the first time a performance was done inside the hall, and not in the village square or the Party office grounds as was previously the practice. Because the hall was small, many people could not get in and it became very crowded. The village had decided to use the hall because of the Oxfam visitors. At this gathering the following people were also present: The District Commissioner, The Division and Ward Party secretaries, The Regional Cultural office representative, the District Cultural officer and all village government officials.

The performance started with songs to welcome the visitors sung by the village primary school. Other songs were on issues of concern at the time, especially the racketeering and black market problems. Other songs were about TSD. Below are presented three of the songs out of the eight performed:

> Karibuni wageni wetu wapendwa
> Kutoka Uingereza, mjisikie nyumbani
> Malya ni mji wa kihistoria
> Mtakaporudi nyumbani Uingereza
> Tutoleeni salaam zetu
> Kwa malikia Elizabeti wa pili
> Karibuni wageni wapendwa.

Translation:
Welcome our dear guests from Britain
Feel at home
Malya is a historical village
When you return to your home Britain
Give our greetings to Queen Elizabeth II
Welcome dear guests.

Watanzania tumekubali lawama za hao walanguzi magendo
Tumesema zamani tukawabembeleza
Na sasa tumefikia mwisho tutumie mabavu
Wanyonyaji wasio na utu
Walisahau kwamba tunayo serkali
Waliturusha rusha
Sasa tumewabana wakamate majembe
Na jasho litawatononeka
Tuliwaomba toka zamani
jamani acheni mateso mnayotupatia
Hawakusikia bidhaa walibana
Zingine wakavusha mpakani kwa mitumbwi na malori
Kuhujumu uchumi

Translation:
We Tanzanians have accepted to confront the problem of racketeers
We tried to plead with them before
But now we have reached the limit of our patience, we shall use force.
Exploiters who have no feelings
They forgot that we have a government
They cheated us again and again
But now we have pinned them down
Let them hold the hoe and sweat
We pleaded with them a long time ago
Please stop causing suffering to people
But they would not listen
They hoarded consumer goods
And transported some of them across the border
In boats and lorries
They are sabotaging our economy.

Tunatoa shukrani kwa wizara ya habari
Tunatoa shukrani kwa Chuo chetu Kikuu

Kutuletea walimu wa sanaa
Mama Mlama pia Chambulikazi
Nae Mama Lihamba pia alikuwepo.

Translation:
We say thank you to the Ministry of Information (and Culture)
We say thank you to our University
For sending us Theatre arts teachers
Madam Mlama and Chambulikazi
And Madam Lihamba was also here.

The play *Walanguzi* was the first to be staged. Its storyline begins with a group of racketeers in Njama village who are selling goods at exorbitant prices. The racketeers are apprehended by the police, taken to the police station, kept in custody and refused bail. Among the racketeers is one woman. Another racketeer goes to Madanganya, a rich businessman and employer of the arrested racketeers, and reports the arrest. Madanganya is very angry with the police especially over the arrest of his girl-friend. He telephones the Regional Party boss who puts him through to the Regional Police commander. The Regional Police commander orders the police commander at the village police station to release the woman racketeer and she is set free. Government officials then come to the bar and they are entertained by Madanganya. Among the officials is the General Manager of the Regional Trading company, responsible for the distribution of food items and other goods. Madanganya introduces his fellow racketeer to the General Manager and the other officials. The General Manager promises them any help they need from the Regional Trading Company. The manager also later discusses his private projects which are to be financed with the money he has received from the racketeers.

At the Regional Trading company, people from the Njama village co-operative shop have come to buy essential goods. They are given inadequate supplies of some and denied others. The racketeers who were drinking with the General Manager also come. They get large amounts of everything. They also give huge bribes to the General Manager. At Njama village co-operative shop a long queue is seen and people are scrambling for goods. Only very few people get anything. Old people and children get hurt in the process. Later at the house of the village shop manager an announcement is heard over the radio that all over the country people are demonstrating to support the President's announcement on the government's decision to crack down on racketeers. The shop manager's wife celebrates this news. A demonstration is also held in Njama village and soon after there are plenty of goods in the village shop. However, there is still a long queue outside this shop because it happens to be the only shop in the village. At closing time the unattended customers fight the shop attendant but in the argument that ensues it is pointed out that one shop is not enough for the village.

Mbio za sakafuni starts in Baba Zakia's house in the morning where they wake up to find that their things have been stolen during the night. Other similar cases are reported by neighbours who come to witness the theft. In fact, people are now scared to walk outside after dark for fear of being attacked. A public meeting is held and a youth officer discusses a government policy to encourage the villagers to start economic projects for the youth. Different views are expressed about the youth including that they are thieves and lazy. During the meeting some young people steal 600 shillings from the elder who is most vocal in his opposition to them. But they are soon apprehended by the people's militia while fighting over their loot.

In the next episode the youth meet to start their economic unit. They elect their leaders and decide on a carpentry project for which the village is ready to donate some equipment. They find out that they actually need a lot more capital than the village can provide. They try to make contributions, but since they do not have any income to begin with, they collect very little money.

In the end they settle for a less expensive project and decide on a coffee shop. To minimise expenses they build the coffee shop themselves. After some time they start to disagree on various issues. Some accuse the leaders of weakness in managing the group and embezzlement of the group's funds. Some decide to quit and demand their money back. In the end the group is divided and half the group leave and those who hang on also leave after some time leaving only the chairman and the secretary. The two are very upset but vow to find a solution because they believe this is the only solution to the youth problem. But how do they solve the problems of getting the project to run? This is the concluding question of the production.

The performance was immediately followed by a discussion on the issues raised and the visitors were invited to contribute their views. Both the shop issue and the youth projects were discussed. A village elder chaired the meeting where the following views were expressed:

(a) Malya was still a long way from making the youth self-reliant. The Party and government at the district level should initiate youth projects for the village.
(b) The youth do try their best to be self-reliant. It is not true to say that they sit idle. (One youth from the audience.)
(c) Can the elders say what they do to instil self-reliance among the youth in Malya? What system did the traditional society use to make sure the youth were meaningfully employed? (Asked by the District Commissioner.)
(d) There was no problem of idle youth in traditional society. The youth worked hard, they spent their time farming and doing other jobs. Maybe it is the formal class-room education which has made them lazy nowadays. (An elder)
(e) The youth are not getting enough material support from the village because the village itself has very little financial power. (Youth)
(f) Can the visitors (Oxfam) explain how the people in Britain solve their problem of youth unemployment? (Village school teacher)
(g) There is a big problem of youth unemployment in England and it is a problem the people in Britain have not managed to solve. (Oxfam visitor)
(h) Oxfam pledges to support programmes that will come out of this Theatre programme. (Oxfam Field Director for Tanzania)
(i) The problems of youth unemployment in Britain are different from those in Tanzania. In Tanzania there is plenty of land so the youth can become self-reliant by engaging in agricultural production. Maybe what they need is agricultural machinery for better production. (Village teacher)

(j) The youth are not loiterers, nor are they bad. The truth is that the youth work hard but they need to unite in order to produce more. (Youth)

(l) The village needs to set up a council of elders which will give advice to the youth about their lives in general. The village has left the youth too much on their own. (Elder)

(m) The youth have already started to work. The theatre group is proof that the youth can organise themselves. They have also started their economic projects in this group. So the youth have already gone some way towards organising. (Elder)

(n) In the play it shows that the youth lose hope easily. They tend to run away from the problems instead of confronting them. (District Commissioner)

(o) The village must remember that many youth used to be petty racketeers. Now that the government has clamped down on racketeers these youths have lost a source of income. The village must work out alternative means of employing them meaningfully. (Elder)

(p) The problem with the present youth is that they want their elders to work for them. It is not like in the old days when the youth worked for their elders. Now the youth have become the elders. (Elder)

(q) The youth have to work first and then if people see their effort they will offer the necessary assistance. (Party Division secretary)

(r) The theatre group must be commended for initiating this discussion about their problems. It is a very positive step towards solving development problems. (District Commissioner)

(s) The women do have problems. (This was in response to a question by one of the visitors who wanted to know whether the women had any problems because they had not spoken.) For example, all my children have left and I have to fend for myself. (An old woman)

(t) The village pledges to support the youth from now on. As a token of that pledge I am starting a fund for the village youth group (the VCG) by contributing this 20 shillings. (This donation was followed by others and 455 shillings were collected on the spot and presented to the chairman of the VCG.)

The discussion on the shop issue was shorter pointing out that it was true that one shop was not enough for Malya. It was suggested that the village should allow other organisations to open more shops. It was said, however, that the Party policy discouraged opening up many shops that are likely to die after a short time. It was for this reason that the initial capital for a village to be allowed to open a shop was put at 10,000 shillings.

The discussion was closed by the elder who was chairing the meeting by thanking all participants in both the performance and the discussion and inviting the visitors to a village lunch which was followed by the performance of several traditional dances in the village square.

Because of the acute shortage of transport the animateur was compelled to go back to Mwanza to catch transport to Dar es Salaam by getting a lift from the Oxfam visitors. The VCG was therefore left to continue working on its own since the project had also come to an end and the animateurs were not scheduled to go back to Malya. There was a feeling of satisfaction on both sides that the VCG which had worked so hard to survive would be able to continue work on their own. A contact by the team in 1987 showed that there was still a group in existence but not enough information was gathered to be included in this section.

CHAPTER 8

Bagamoyo Popular Theatre Workshop 1983

Influenced by the Popular Theatre work by the University of Dar es Salaam team and their participation in the Murewa Popular Theatre workshop, the Bagamoyo college of art decided to launch its own First Popular Theatre workshop in 1983. The college which is a training centre for the country's cultural workers is situated in the small, historical town of Bagamoyo which was an important port for the slave trade. The workshop was held in Bagamoyo town itself and became the first Popular Theatre workshop in an urban setting in Tanzania.

The objectives of the workshop were to train the students of the college in the Popular Theatre process as well as to involve the Bagamoyo residents in the use of theatre to discuss and analyse their problems. Thirty-five students and ten members of staff participated in the exercise. Animateurs from the University of Dar es Salaam, those who had run the Malya project, were invited to participate as resource persons. Cultural officers and youth leaders from the Bagamoyo district offices also participated.[1]

Background to Bagamoyo

Bagamoyo lies on the coast of the Indian ocean and it was thus a port for the slave trade, but it also had other trade links with countries to the East of the African continent. It has a long history of Arab influence on its economy and general way of life. It was one of the bulwarks of the feudal system which showed great resistance to the introduction of the Ujamaa mode of production. Although the Arabs have left, the local people are holding on to

---

1. Materego, G. 1983, *Ripoti ya washa ya Sanaa kwa maendeleo ya Jamii—Chuo Cha Sanaa Bagamoyo*, (unpublished).

their acquired Arabic cultural practices, especially the Islamic religion and feudal economic and social relations.

Many Bagamoyo residents still live as serfs working for a few landlords who own coconut plantations and fishing boats. Those few who own the means of production are looked upon as *Mwinyi* (lords). They spend most of their time praying or playing *bao* because manual work lowers their dignity. The same goes for the members of their families, especially the women who spend their lives in seclusion. The rest of the community slave for these *mwinyis* for returns not enough to give them two meals a day.

Efforts by the government to mobilise the people against this economic structure have been hampered by the enormous control the *mwinyis* have over the lower classes. People are not only economically dependent on the *mwinyis* who employ them as agricultural labourers, fishermen, and traders for their coconut or fish, but they also suffer a social and cultural domination boardering on awe for the *mwinyis*. The *mwinyis* are believed to possess deadly witchcraft powers which they can wield against those interfering with their interests. The majority of the population is therefore paralysed into silence in fear of their lives. The fishermen, most of whom are employees of the *mwinyis* who own the fishing boats, would not offend a *mwinyi* because they believe they need the good will of the *mwinyi* to return safely from the sea. The political will to develop the area has not been enough to counter these fears and move people to meaningful action. There are informal suggestions that real political power in Bagamoyo is with the *mwinyis* rather than the official representatives of the state.

In Bagamoyo people do not generally farm large acreages or build very good houses, even if they had the ability to do so, in fear of offending the *mwinyis*. In spite of the large incomes the *mwinyis* themselves realise by exploiting their employees, they often live in poor houses giving the town a very ancient and poor appearance. Most people, therefore, are forced to depend on the market for their food which is often too expensive for their meagre incomes from wage labour or petty trade. This situation presents a complex and difficult background to development planning. Although recently there have been some signs of increased agricultural production through specific government campaigns, the improvement of the lower classes is very slight. This was, indeed, a difficult and very challenging context in which to set a Popular Theatre workshop.

Research and information gathering

Due to the sensitive nature of the area it was considered wise to seek a public political patronage through staging an official opening at the town square, presided over by the District Commissioner. In his opening speech, the District Commissioner explained at length the close relationship between the society and art since the pre-capitalist era. He then outlined the development problems facing Bagamoyo. He pointed out that historically Bagamoyo was a centre of civilisation because of its trade links with the rest of the country and the world. Surprisingly though, he remarked, now the Bagamoyo residents are not willing to participate in development activities. He said that many residents are still under the influence of Arabic feudal practices, as a result of which they just sit around and play *bao*. He called upon the residents to look into and analyse the frighteningly rampant belief in witchcraft and its consequences.

The workshop participants were then divided into three groups to cover three different areas of the town. Prior arrangements had been made to involve local dance groups from these three areas to form the artistic core groups. Only one group of *Mdundiko* turned up. The other two groups apparently boycotted the workshop at the last minute because of a suspicion that they would not be paid for their participation. In fact when at the end of the workshop the *Mdundiko* group was not paid conflict erupted among the members and the group leader was accused of cheating. Here was a manifestation of the possible impact of urban culture on Popular Theatre practice. The workshop groups were therefore forced to adopt their own tactics in maximising the participation of the local population. It was decided also to try different forms. One group was to work on dance and mime, the second on story-telling and the third on puppetry. Puppetry is not a popular theatre form in Tanzania, but because of its success elsewhere it was decided to try out its possibilities with a Tanzanian audience.

Finding out the problems of the people

Let us look in detail at the work of one group, group B, of which the author was a member. The team had fifteen members including staff and students of Bagamoyo college. Its area of operation was known as Majengo and it was one of the places whose local dance group refused to participate.

The team was too big to move together. It was therefore divided into groups of twos and threes. Without the participation of the local residents as researchers, the team had no other alternative but to use the conventional research methodology of moving from house to house interviewing people, chatting and discussing some issues. An effort was made to cover all age groups and both sexes. Although it was not easy to get the process going because of the "stranger" status of the animateurs, the popularity of the college due to their frequent public performances helped to break many barriers. Many of the students were known to the residents by their stage characters and people were delighted to meet them in real life. Otherwise the urban setting made the community less of a single unit as was the case in the villages. The suspicion of strangers and the fear of witchcraft did not help much. Neither did the seclusion of women. All these setbacks though did not prevent the team from coming up with some problems of concern to the area. The major problems were outlined as follows:

(a)   Inadequate food supply resulting from low food production in the area, feudal attitudes that made people look down upon farming; laziness and land shortage.

(b)   Poor quality of education characterised by a high truancy rate, lack of co-operation between parents and teachers, parents demeaning formal education, lack of basic educational facilities and children being lured away from school by petty business such as selling fish.

(c)   The leaders do not make a proper follow up of development problems and give too many unfulfilled promises.

(d)   High unemployment among the youth, both boys and girls result in abnormal behaviour among the youth including bang-smoking and loitering. It seemed the educational system does not adequately prepare the children for meaningful employment in the village after primary school.

(e) A feudal socio-economic structure is still in existence. The Party and government leaders are afraid of the *mwinyis* and therefore cannot implement plans to uproot feudalism.
(f) There is a very entrenched belief in witchcraft. The witchcraft is also tied to feudalism.

Because of the ineffective participation of the local residents in the research process, it was difficult to involve them in a collective analysis of the data. Instead this was done mostly by the animateur. It was decided to leave further analysis to the theatre performance stage where it was hoped the local residents would participate more effectively.

The theatre performance process

The animateurs chose the primary school playground in Majengo for the theatrical performance. For three days the team performed under a big mango tree. The session started with drumming and dancing by the animateurs which attracted the local residents. Then the rehearsals started whereby the team collectively created a story that attempted to portray the major problem of Bagamoyo area: feudalism and its effects.

The performance was based on the story-telling form popular in Bagamoyo as well as in other parts of the country. Dramatic skits and mimed action were integrated into the narration. The narrators tried their best to incorporate the audience into the performance by asking questions during the narration and incorporating their contributions. During the rehearsals the animateurs also tried to incorporate audience participation. It became apparent that the audience was interested in the theme but were very cautious of what to say. Some looked on and walked away without comment. Others, however, especially the fishermen recognised their plight and participated in the discussion. They were, however, unwilling to take an active part in the actual dramatisation, mimes or narrations. Most of the acting was thus done by the animateurs.

Some discussion revealed that the local people were afraid of the *mwinyis'* reactions to the performance. But their limited participation could also have been a result of their getting used to have performances done for them by the college of art. To them this was just another event where the college artists had come to perform for them. The urban setting did not help much either, because the people are not closely linked to each other as would be the case in the villages. To perform or not was an individual decision rather than a social obligation.

The final performance, however, did manage to get some amount of audience participation. The text of the performance is presented below.

Narrator:	Paukwa! (A formal way of starting a storytelling session in Tanzania. It means once upon a time.)
Audience:	Pakawa (There was)
Narrator:	Hadithi hadithi (a story a story)
Audience:	Hadithi njoo (Let the story come)
Narrator:	Well, once upon a time there was
Audience:	Yes go on
Narrator:	There was a village by the name of Chitandi. Yeees that village was rich in every aspect. It was a village of plenty. The villagers were rich for two reasons. They had plenty of land and secondly the village was on the coast. Yes. Do you see the coast? (Indicating the ocean in Bagamoyo.) Yes. So everyone went to work in the morning. This one took the hoe, that one the fishing nets to the sea and the other one …

(A mime on various occupations in the village. The mime is done to a traditional worksong.)

Narrator: It went on like that, every morning, everybody to his or her duties. Those who went to the farm brought home cassava, potatoes also maize. Those who entered the sea came out with fish. Yes and they exchanged the goods. Famine was unknown to them and if at all there was shortage of food then maybe it was due to an epidemic but otherwise there was never famine.

So days went by and days went by. One day they left their homes ... yes ... on the way to the sea. When they arrived at the shore they were now ready to set their fishing gear into the sea. Oh' suddenly, looking over the water they saw a vessel coming, a vessel coming, and it is coming very fast. Yes, is the wind blowing this way? Is it blowing this way? No, it is blowing out to sea, it is blowing towards where we are going to fish. But that's strange, that vessel is coming this way. They are all gaping at it.

(A song which everybody joins in.)

        Kile nini kile nini
        Kile ng'ambo ya bahari
        Kile nini kile nini
        Kile ng'ambo ya bahari

Translation:
What is that what is that
That over the sea
What is that what is that
That over the sea?

Narrator:	The vessel arrived at shore and anchored. Oh' our friends walked backwards to hide and peep to see what people or things would come out. It was strange that the wind was going but the vessel kept coming. Yes. All of a sudden they saw strange creatures getting out. My mother! and their luggage, they put on shore, they go in, they come out. Then they ran fast back home, abandoning their fishing nets, everything, they ran home.
Voice 1:	What is it?
Voice 2:	Ooh' we have been invaded.
Voice 3:	Yeee my mother, we have been invaded.
Voice 4:	Who? Where are the children?
Voice 5:	Have we given the gods our offering this year?

Voice 2:	No.
Voice 1:	Send a child to find out what is happening.
Voice 6:	I am not going, not me.
Voice 4:	You men are afraid, so you want to send a woman. No?
Voice 3:	No before deciding on anything let us send two of our young warriors.
Voice 2:	Very well said. Let us have one.
Voice 5:	No this is voluntary. So let us have two volunteers. Let them volunteer themselves, for the love of their country. Let us have a warrior, a hero.
Youth 1:	I will go.
Youth 2:	And so will I.

(applause from the rest)

Narrator:	Those devils. They are everywhere on the beach. They are seated in a circle, they are drinking, the others are eating. Look! They are talking. The young people were surprised. Yes these devils are talking. So they started running back home. At home everybody's heart is beating faster, will our children disappear? All eyes to the sea, towards which their children had disappeared.
Youth 1:	Did you hear? We went. We went. On the way I felt like coming back but he said no, let's have all our courage. Let's go. So we went. Before reaching that point, first we saw that big, I don't know, vessel. It is big and hanging like this, it is very beautiful. The way I see it that belongs to the devils.
Youth 2:	We took a closer look, white people, white, their hair is a little white but they have skin like people.
Voice 1:	Devils, those are devils.
Voice 5:	Friends we have been invaded by a curse so I think the only way is to give offerings to our ancestors.

Voice 3: Right, right, I agree.
(Song and mime of ancestral worship and offering.)
Holile holile holile holile
holile holile
holile holile
holile holile
Digambe difugo dikufugize
Holile holile
Igambe misimu ikufugize
holile holile

Translation:
Rest in peace rest in peace
Ask the shrine to make peace
Ask the ancestors to make peace
Rest in peace.

Narrator: After that our friends went back to their homes. Yes. I tell you, I am even scared to tell you. Things took a bad turn, a real bad turn. Those creatures, instead of going away like we prayed, like our friends in Chitandi prayed, they started to settle in Chitandi. To the south, the north, at the centre of Chitandi. Oh' they spread all over. Our friend in Chitandi, when he goes out in the morning and looks around, sees them walking, so he goes back inside and only peeps through the window. But one of our friends from Chitandi, this fellow come forward. We do not know what he did.

Kibao: Alah ah alah laila'
Hey don't make me laugh. Why are you running away? Don't you know me, your husband?

Wife: No, don't follow me. What are you wearing?
Kibao: I got these clothes from those foreigners.
Wife: Those devils?
Kibao: They are not devils.

Wife:	Leave me alone. These are devils and now today you are also a devil.
Kibao:	Don't touch me, you will make my clothes dirty.
Wife:	But my hands are clean.
Kibao:	No go and wash them first.
Child 1:	He looks like a devil (runs out). Come and see how my father is dressed, hurry.
Child 2:	What is he wearing?
Child 1:	Come.
Child 3:	I will go and tell my father.
Narrator:	The situation continued like that, the children were afraid of him the wife was afraid of him and so were some of the other people in Chitandi. But some were curious to know how he got these clothes. So he told them, 'Look if you want these clothes just go to the people they will give them to you. They mean no harm, they simply give.' So a procession began going for clothes. Soon Chitandi was divided into two, the foreigners and the local people. But soon the foreigners started dominating. They expanded their farms, they imported different things. But do you know who was doing all the work?
Voice:	We don't know.
Voice:	Were the foreigners many?
Narrator:	Who knows who was doing the work?
Voice:	Us.
Voice:	Who?
Voice:	The local Chitandi people.
Narrator:	You are right my friend. It was the Chitandi people who did the farming. Even me, they took my farm by force.
Voice:	They took your farm?
Narrator:	Yes, the Chitandi people did the farming for them. They were given pieces to work on, measured according to steps. So many steps up to there, you finish then you come and you are

paid. In the evening he takes his pay but his wife gets no clothes, only food. This went on for years, the plantation got bigger, our friends in Chitandi started to mix with the foreigners, got used to them and some of them were even given jobs of responsibility. They were told 'You oversee your relatives while they are working. When this work is done I will give you the piece of land in reward. It has already been cleared and you will plant what you want. You will be overseer for my farm while at the same time looking after your own farm. Is that OK?' 'Yes' he agreed and he became the overseer and work continued.

The situation became worse in the village. As the years passed the overseer commanding their uncles, aunts and cousins to work. They did not do any work. In the end all the overseers in Chitandi said 'Hey listen'.

(A meeting of overseers)

Voice:	Let us oust these foreigners from this land and then we can take over the land.
Voice:	That's right.
Voice:	And when they run away to their own country, we take over their farms.
Voice:	Excuse me, I have just come, what is it you said?
Voice:	We have called you to say let us unite and oust these foreigners.
Voice:	And then we take over their farms.
Voice:	You mean these white people?
Voice:	You mean my landlord too?
Voice:	Yes all of them.
Voice:	Not mine.
Voice:	This is not their land.
Voice:	No I won't do it, he gave me a big farm.
Voice:	Are you satisfied?
Voice:	But we are many. Let us oust them.

Voice:	No way. My landlord has a thing which brings down the monkeys from the coconut palms. I saw it myself. You think you will ever manage to chase him away?
Voice:	Do not be afraid of that. We shall surprise him and the others.
Voice:	No no do not touch my landlord.
Voice:	He is the one who shall go first, we shall destroy him. Listen, after destroying him we shall own that land and then we shall make the people continue working for us. We shall be the landlords.
Voice:	But then we have to mobilise all the people to be on our side, first.
Voice:	(To the audience) Listen everybody. We want to oust the white people so that we can own our land. What do you say?

(A celebration to mark the ousting of the foreigners done to dance and music.)

>Wananchi wa kijiji tuna furaha leo
>Wananchi wa kijiji tuna furaha leo
>
>*Translation:*
>The villagers are very happy today

Narrator:	All the residents of Chitandi are celebrating their victory in ousting the foreigners. The few remaining are only those you know who tried to marry our grandmothers, others were left in the stomach and some small children. Yes. Just the remnants. So the days went on and on. One day early in the morning they said OK this is the day. What we agree upon is here. Let us go to those overseers so that we can distribute the land to everybody. We need to start working on our pieces.
Voice:	We have come for our pieces of land.
Voice:	I also want mine with the coconut palms.
Voice:	No, I want the coconut palm too.

Voice:	So do I.
Voice:	Hey listen.
Voice:	This piece here is mine.
Voice:	First let us ask ourselves the question who came up with the idea for us to fight?
Voice:	Everybody.
Voice:	Who was in the frontline?
Voice:	Everybody.
Voice:	Don't say everybody. I was in the frontline so this house is all mine.
Voice:	No way.
Voice:	Who says no?
Voice:	I say no.
Voice:	We say no.
Voice:	Now listen, from now on you shall be under us. You will continue to work on the land like you did for the landlords. You shall work, we shall only increase your wages.
Voice:	No we shall not farm.
Voice:	I shall do it.
Voice:	No way.
Voice:	(shouting) Listen, you shall work.
Voice:	No no. What is this?
Voice:	You shall work. Whoever refuses, his throat will be slashed. Overseer continue with the work immediately.

(Work done on the farm to the accompaniment of a worksong.)

Tulime lime tukale mboga

Translation:
Let us dig and we shall eat vegetables

Narrator:	The overseers held fast to the coconut palms plantations, small businesses were started. Soon their names were changed. Yes even the names. They changed their habits, their religion, their style of clothing. Yes. They became different, calling themselves foreign names. Very dangerous, I tell you, danger followed

danger. They started preventing their children from going to school, instead they gave them fish to trade. Some are at the beach acting as overseers for the fishermen. The situation became worse and worse. Our friends continued to expand. Yes the situation became really bad. Years went on, years went on. Yes.

Shall I continue narrating this story or not?

Audience: Continue.
Narrator: Shall I continue or not?
Audience: Please continue.
Narrator: Days passed and days passed, yes days became weeks became months and months years. And all those days life at Chitandi was simply toiling and suffering. You know what happened one day? One man by the name of Selemani. Yes look at him coming from the house. 'Look at how thin we have become.' So he and his fellow fishermen decided that whatever fish they get they will keep. Some of it they will use for food. Some they will sell and pool the money which they will later use to buy their own fishing boats plus their own fishing nets. They are tired of being exploited. Yes. So as the days passed their fund grew and grew. So they send one of them to the government to get a loan to supplement their own money. The fellow succeeded. But he was told 'This is a loan which must be paid back in three years'. OK. So they bought all the fishing gear and brought it to the village. Mmmmh, do you know what happened?

Village crier: People of Chitandi listen. Things are happening, great things. Come to the shore. Everybody come to the shore. Today things are happening.

Voice: Thank you for turning up. Do you see that which is in front of you?

Voice: A fishing boat.

Voice:	A fishing boat?
Voice:	Yes, yes.
Voice:	Yes a fishing boat. The fruits of your labour and contributions. But we have a debt which we have to pay back in three years time.
Voice:	It is OK. We shall pay it.
Voice:	Now I take this opportunity to invite the guest of honour, our village chairman to inaugurate our fishing boat. Our own fishing boat. And we want him to give it a name.

(applauding)

Voice:	And I give this fishing boat the name *Ushirika* (Co-operation). And let us push it into the water now so that it starts work immediately.
	Up with co-operation!
Audience:	Up, Up, Up

(Worksong performed to the movement of the fishing boat and rowing)

>Ae tuitwike kalanda katuzana
>aee tuitike kalanda katuzana
>kalanda katuzana
>Ae tuitike kalanda katuzana.

Narrator:	Shall I continue or not?
Audience:	Continue.
Narrator:	Have you seen the fishing boat?
Audience:	Yeees.
Narrator:	Yes: OK. People are making too much noise. I can't continue. My story ends here.

(Very loud applause)

Post-performance discussion

Not enough rapport was struck between the animateurs and the audience to sustain a meaningful and lively discussion after the performance. A few people commented that the performance depicted their reality and agreed that their problems were much tied to the *mwinyis*. But there was some unwillingness to go deeper into the problem. Slowly the audience walked away, discussing among themselves views that they probably did not feel safe to air publicly. It was the impression of the animateurs that the fear of witchcraft was at the core of such a reaction. It was strongly felt that the performance should have dealt also with the witchcraft issue. Witchcraft was not given importance here because another workshop group was handling that. It was felt, however, that witchcraft was tied to all the problems in Bagamoyo.

The workshop eventually decided to stage two of the workshop performances at the open air theatre of the college of art. Because the Bagamoyo residents were used to attending theatre performances at this theatre it was hoped that many people would come and a post-performance discussion would supplement the failures of the residential discussions. Sure enough, a big audience turned up and the two performances were presented.

The storyline of the other group's performance involved a family that migrated to a village. Unlike the local residents, they work hard on a big piece of land and get a good harvest. They invite their neighbours to celebrate their big harvest. Then the witches meet and plan on how to destroy this family. The father is bitten by a snake on the farm. The neighbours call a traditional doctor who tells him that the snake was sent to him because of his good harvest. He warns him not to engage in agriculture otherwise he will die. The family turns to petty business which leads to their impoverishment. In the end, they decide to move to another village. But other people come to persuade them not to .... They point out that every person who comes to live in this village moves after a short time. Moving will not solve the problem and, therefore, they must find solutions to the problem instead of running away. They decide to venture into collective farming. They mobilise all the poor people to be members of this co-operative farm. They set out to see whether the so called witches would attack them as a co-operative and in unity.

The performance provoked a very lively debate. Somehow, the Bagamoyo residents felt it safe to discuss their problems within the confines of the college of art. There was general agreement that the belief in witchcraft was rampant in Bagamoyo. This negatively affected development efforts in the area. Even though more people from other parts of Tanzania now reside in Bagamoyo, it has not diluted the belief in witchcraft. This was one reason behind the constant shortage of food supplies, it was argued.

Suggestions on how to solve the problem zeroed in on the need for the government to pursue development projects on a collective rather than an individual basis. It should institute such projects as collective farms where individuals would not feel vulnerable. In the end the people would realise that there was no witchcraft involved in their development problems.

It was also pointed out that there was a need for a closer co-operation between the leaders and the people of the lower classes. The Party and government leaders tended to strike alliances with the *mwinyis* as a result of which they do not cater for the interests of the common people. This had created apathy among the poor, often interpreted as laziness by the leaders. This apathy could be eliminated if the leaders made an effort to understand the problems also from the people's point of view.

Follow-up action

Because of the problems to get the people to participate as a community, it was difficult to come up with specific suggestions for follow-up action. The workshop had to settle only for the discussions with the audience and hope that at least some awareness had been created through the performances and the limited discussion and that such awareness could lead to some action.

Despite the shortcomings the workshop did score some success especially in relation to its objective of training the students of the college in the Popular Theatre process. In fact Bagamoyo college has now introduced Popular Theatre as a teaching subject. Also between 1984 and 1986, the college has conducted other workshops in Kerege, Kilomo, Pande, and Zinga villages in Bagamoyo district. Some students and staff of the college have also participated in Popular Theatre workshops organised by the University of Dar es Salaam. Students and staff of the Bagamoyo College of Art have participated in the Msoga and Mkambalani workshops organised by the University of Dar es Salaam.

CHAPTER 9
Msoga Popular Theatre Workshop 1985

In January 1985, a Popular Theatre workshop was conducted in Msoga village in Bagamoyo district of the Coast region. This workshop was organised under the auspices of the African Participatory Research Network (APRN) in the realisation that there was a strong relationship between Popular Theatre and participatory research. Both are committed to the promotion of the participation of the members of the community in the development process. Participatory research promotes development through popular education, and it furthers a research methodology which aims to increase the awareness of people and to mobilise them for collective action. Popular Theatre is, therefore, a relevant practice within the Participatory Research process in that it goes beyond research to concretise the findings into a public expression of people's own feelings and it has follow-up action.[1]

Msoga was to serve as a continuation of the Popular Theatre practice, building on the experience gained in Malya and Bagamoyo. The team of animateurs, the same people as those involved in Malya and Bagamoyo, wished to improve on the Popular Theatre process by using Msoga to try and overcome the shortcomings of the previous workshops.

Background to Msoga

Msoga is an Ujamaa village located about ten kilometres off the main road that goes to Moshi from Chalinze. The residents are mostly of the Kwere ethnic group and the population at the time of the workshop was about 700. The low population is a sign of

---

1. Chambulikazi, E. 1983, *Report on Msoga Popular Theatre Workshop*, (unpublished), University of Dar es Salaam.

the village dying. At its peak in the late 1970s it had twice the present number of people.

Msoga's history has been troubled by conflicts with the government dating back to the mid 1970s villagisation programme when the Msoga residents refused to move to a new village. The fight to remain in Msoga, whose land was more fertile and whose water resources were more permanent than the area the government had earmarked for them, led to a physical confrontation with the villagisation officials. In the end the villagers won and stayed in Msoga, but in the process they lost the primary school and the political goodwill of the leaders. The villagers are very proud of this background, a fact displayed in their talk and even in the names of dance leaders. "Zaulole" (come and see), for example, is a reference to the fact that they have survived and will continue to survive the struggle for their existence.

Despite their history of militancy, Msoga suffers most of the problems of underdevelopment. Production is very low and apathy has replaced creativity and initiative. Poverty is so rampant that many people cannot afford two meals a day. People seem to hang on to life in the village because they have no alternative. The irony of it is the abundance of fertile land and the permanent water supply. There is a river and a dam that was constructed in 1955.

The Kwere cultural traditions are very much alive in spite of the vulnerability of the area to outside influence, due to their coastal location. Traditional dance is very popular as seen in the existence of several permanent and well-organised dance groups in the village. These included Bigililo, a women's group whose performances consisted of dance and dramatic skits woven into the dance; Chizalia, a mixed group, and Mkwajungoma, a youth dance group. These groups participated in both the traditional Kwere cultural ceremonies such as initiations and weddings and the more contemporary events related to national political celebrations. While at the village they continued the traditional practice of portraying social problems. During the political events they followed the same trend as with other groups in the country of toeing the Party line. Unlike many groups, though, their artist activities were wider than the political events. In fact the Bigililo group had won much fame in the district for its performances also at traditional social occasions.

The Msoga performances

The workshop team of animateurs consisted of fifteen people, the biggest group ever in Tanzanian Popular Theatre practice. This included four from the University of Dar es Salaam, five students of the Bagamoyo College of Art who participated as part of their training, one from Butimba College of Art, three cultural officers from the Coast region and two guest artists from the neighbouring countries of Uganda and Zambia. An additional person also participated as organiser from the APRN.

As was the case with Malya, the workshop could not start immediately with the research stage because the village had prepared their own programme to kick off the workshop. So the first day was spent watching and participating in theatre performances by the three village dance groups mentioned earlier. The Bigililo group started with a dance to welcome the guests. After several social themes including one of the bad neighbour, the woman who steals meat from another woman, and is then caught and greatly ridiculed. While some of the dancers took up the dramatic roles, the rest remained part of the cast by continuously stamping their feet to the dance rhythm.

Different groups from the village put on performances. The content of the play (Mkwajungoma) performed by the youth dealt with issues such as love, drinking and other social problems. One of their skits was about a woman who was by herself and feeling hungry she cooked some food. But because there is not enough food to share she decides to hide it. When her husband finds out he beats her up. The Chizalia group did a dance which originated from Upogoro in Mahenge district and was originally known as Silanga. They also did a skit on Nguvukazi, the theme of what was then a national campaign on human deployment. One of their dance songs was on the problems of the dispensary in Msoga where medicine was not available. The song was a plea to the guests, the animateurs to assist in solving this problem. After the skits, dancing went on the whole day, and the participation was very enthusiastic.

Although this programme was not designed by the workshop team it offered a very good starting point not only for getting both sides to identify with each other but also to introduce the team to the artistic background of Msoga as well as giving them a glimpse of the problems to be dealt with during the workshop. It was decided, therefore, that the local theatre groups would form the core groups for the Popular Theatre process. The team members were divided into three and joined the local artists of Bigililo, Chizalia and Mkwajungoma. The rest of the villagers were free to join any of the three groups.

Information gathering

On the following day, the three groups set out for research and information gathering which covered the whole geographical area of the village, visiting different households and talking to different age groups and covering both sexes. The process of data collection was supposed to involve both the animateurs and the villagers. However, the animateurs later discovered that there was a problem in that some members of the local dance group were cell leaders, and they tried to influence the information which the villagers gave during the research process. There were cases of the leaders sometimes winking at the villagers when certain questions were asked. Also the asking of questions was left mostly to the animateurs, and the leaders were quick to come up with the answers before the other villagers could say anything. This suggested a lack of trust in the animateurs by the villagers and a feeling that the villagers were hiding something. To rectify the situation, the animateurs had to device ways of avoiding this control of information. Informal information gathering through chats or drinking beer at the local beer places was resorted to.

The following problems were identified:

(a) There was a great need for agricultural inputs, especially a tractor because, the villagers argued, the soil was very heavy and not enough acreage could be worked with the hand hoe. Other problems related to agriculture included insufficient supplies of hand hoes and fertilizers and bad transport because the road was impassable during the rainy season.

(b) There were no adequate health services. There was no clinic, and pregnant women had to walk many kilometres to the clinic in Lugoba. A health centre was under construction but it had been started eight years ago, and was far from completion. The health services at the dispensary were also bad because of the negative attitudes of the medical personnel and a shortage of drugs.
(c) There was a big shortage of educational material including book and desks. Poor examination performance at the school as well as pregnancies among school girls were also issues of great concern.
(d) Although the village had plenty of water from natural sources, the water was unhygienic and there was no tap water.
(e) The development tax recently introduced by the government was a burden to many people whose income was not big enough to afford the tax.
(f) Supply of essential commodities was inadequate. Sugar, rice and flour were hardly ever available in the village shop. Instead people had to go to town in search of these items.
(g) Leadership in the village was weak and old-fashioned.
(h) Unwanted pregnancies even among schoolgirls were on the increase.
(i) The grain mill in the village was breaking down, and this very often forced people to walk long distances to other mills.

A public discussion was held at the village square to analyse these problems. There were about three hundred people present. The discussion centred around the problems of agriculture, health and education.

On agriculture the village leaders championed the need for a tractor arguing that this would dig deep into the heavy soil and take good care of the weeds that were difficult to uproot with a hand hoe. Also the acreage would increase and production improve. An experience was quoted of when in 1976 a government tractor was brought to the village for one season free of charge. The village then cultivated 300 hectares of food crops and got a good harvest. But the tractors did not come back and production fell again.

There were also complaints that, like in other Ujamaa villages, the people were expected to work on too many farms at the same time. There was the Ujamaa farm, and the *Bega kwa bega*, which were individual farms but located next to the farms of other villagers so that they could be worked on communally, and then they had still other individual farms. The week is therefore divided up between these farms which does not give enough time to each farm as well as straining the farmers. It was also pointed out that the Ujamaa farm was located very far from the village and people wasted both time and energy walking to the farm.

It was also reported that a week prior to the workshop there was a rumour of the sighting of a very big snake at the Ujamaa farm. The snake was so huge that one person could not kill it. The services of a snake charmer was, therefore, sought for and on a Sunday the whole village went out with the snake charmer but there was no snake. Anyway, now nobody wanted to go near the farm because they were afraid of the snake. During the discussion, however, the village chairman asked why the snake chose to go to the Ujamaa farm and then only during the rainy season. This led to the realisation that the snake rumour and the snake charming exercise in reality represented the villagers' resistance to work on the Ujamaa farm.

On the health issue it was noted that the UNICEF-funded clinic had taken eight years to build, and was not finished yet. The village had tried its best to see the district authorities about this, but in vain. There were allegations of misappropriation of cement and roofing material at the district and village levels. The need to resolve the shortage of drugs at the existing dispensary was also emphasised, especially in relation to pregnant women.

The unhealthy water created a heated argument, as a result of which some of the animateurs went to the river to see the condition of the water for themselves. The argument was that the water was unclean because of the dam that had been built many years ago and which had accumulated a lot of dirt which affected the whole river. If the dam was cleaned the water would be clean. Others argued that the dam was so old having been built in the 1950s, that it could not be cleaned because it had accumulated too much silt and dirt. It was also mentioned that the diseases in the village were not only due to the unclean water but also to the lack of latrines in many households. This issue was, however, glossed over. The people did not show much interest in discussing. It was not clear whether this was due to shyness or whether it was simply not important to them.

On education there was a strong feeling that the teachers should be held responsible for pregnancies among schoolgirls. The teachers argued back saying it was the parents' fault because they do things that children are not supposed to see. Parents have bad habits which in turn corrupt the children. Others thought this was a result of the new times. It was also pointed out that in the old days girls were brought up to be married with a person in the village but now it was no longer the same, and girls could therefore misbehave. The girls were also blamed for not co-operating with the parents to help them. For example, many of them refused to name the men who made them pregnant.

The popular theatre performance

The three groups went to different places to conduct rehearsals. The rehearsals were public enabling anybody in the village to participate. In all the groups passers-by and members of the community joined the artistic creations. The three dance groups chose to work with three different topics. The Bigililo group chose to deal with the pregnancy issue, Chizalia with village leadership, and the Mkwajungoma with the development tax. The dance forms of these groups were to form the basis of the artistic expressions. In fact the animateurs were struck by the Msoga artistic form seen on the first day where dance and dramatic skits were effectively combined to produce an artistic form unique to Msoga. The theatre groups in the village seemed to have established this format of performance which was well received by their audience. The animateurs felt that the format offered a new form to experiment with in the Popular Theatre process.

It should be mentioned here that story-telling was also very much part of the Popular Theatre workshop at Msoga but came spontaneously during the breaks in the workshop timetable. The workshop faced a problem, also faced by all previous workshops, of how to follow a practical timetable. It was difficult to come up with a timetable that could fit all the activities of the villagers, co-ordination was difficult because of the nature of life in the village. In Msoga many hours were spent waiting for people to gather.

During these periods of waiting, however, there were story-telling sessions that developed spontaneously in order to pass the time. The villagers who arrived earlier and the animateurs participated in these sessions. One great story-teller was Mzee Petri Mgweno who seemed to have an unending stream of stories. The story-telling sessions were also filled with a lot of singing and laughter because Mzee Petri was also full of humour. Other villagers also participated as story-tellers.

During these story-telling sessions a story was told of contemporary Msoga where a big man came and requested to be a member of the village and get a farm. He sent a government tractor to work on his farm and then asked the villagers to plant his farm for him because he was busy, then he asked them to weed it and to harvest it after which the big man came and collected his harvest, and he has never been seen in the village since. This was told in the story-telling mode and made to appear like it was a story but it was a true event and the villagers used the story to ridicule the Party leader who had done this to them.

After four days of working in the separate group, the four groups came together for a public performance. This was designed to be a mini-performance to give a chance to the groups to get a feedback from the rest of the community. Then they went back to group work and reassembled after one day for the final show.

The Bigililo group's performance

They began with an introductory song to the accompaniment of which they danced into the performing area. Then followed a song on the pregnancy problem which had the following text:

>Watoto wa siku hizi kwa uhuni wameshinda
>Kutoka hapa nyumbani nadhani kenda shule
>Kumbe kapakia daladala
>Nimepokea barua inatoka CCM

Eti mwanao kapata mimba
Namwuliza mwanangu anisema niambae'we mama usinijue'
Namchukua mwanangu safari ya CCM
Nimefika CCM wazee kumwuliza
mimba hii ni ya nani
Mimba hii ya upepo
Mambo yako sikubali namshitaki mzazi
Anakwenda mahakama
Kusikia mahakama mtoto kapata woga
Mmemtaja Mgweno naye akakataa
Mzazi kasikitika hakimu nipe barua
Namshitaki Mgweno kaniharibia mwanangu
Asha na Mgweno wote mkafungwe
Chitendo chomtendile, wote mkafungwe.

Translation:
Children of these days have excelled in being loose
They leave home, I assume they have gone to school
But they have boarded *daladala* (public buses in town)
I have received a letter from CCM
That my daughter is pregnant
I ask my daughter, she tells me to get lost,
'mother leave me alone'
I take my daughter to CCM
I arrive there, CCM elders ask her who made her pregnant
She says it is the wind
'I don't accept that, I will sue your parent'
CCM will go to court
When she hears about going to court she is scared
She mentions one Mgweno
I ask Mgweno who denies it
The parent is annoyed
Mr magistrate, give me an injunction I am taking Mgweno to court
He has destroyed my daughter
Asha and Mgweno, both of you should go to jail
For what you have done, both of you should go to jail.

After the song sung by a duet to the accompaniment of instrumental music of drums and ankle bells the dancers performed the *bigililo* dance. It is a dance that employs very intricate foot-work. When the song comes to an abrupt stop the skits start.

CCM Chairman: Soldier, go and arrest Mgweno and take him to court.

(Scene at the court, Asha, the girl, her mother and Mgweno at the court.)

Magistrate:	You are Mgweno. Is that true?
Mgweno:	Yes.
Magistrate:	Do you know this girl?
Mgweno:	I know her.
Magistrate:	What is her name?
Mgweno:	Asha.
Magistrate:	Do you know this woman?
Mgweno:	She is a village mother.
Magistrate:	What relationship does she have to that girl?
Mgweno:	She is her daughter.
Magistrate:	Asha. Do you know this man?
Asha:	Yes I know him. He is my lover and he has made me pregnant.
Magistrate:	OK Mgweno, you are accused of making Asha pregnant. Do you plead guilty?
Mgweno:	I do not agree.
Magistrate:	Why don't you agree?
Mgweno:	First I am an old man how can I impregnate her. These girls they take people's money.
Magistrate:	Asha do you have any evidence?
Asha:	My first evidence is the prenatal clinic card. We go together to the clinic. My second evidence he has a black spot on his left buttock.
Magistrate:	It is claimed that you have a black spot on your left leg and this clinic card shows that you are registered as the father.
Mgweno:	These are the girls who take people's money then they write any name on the card. These are the schoolgirls. They are notorious.
Magistrate:	Court assessors, do you have anything to say before the judgement?

Court Assessor:	In my opinion, this man is guilty. For a man of his age to do such a shameful thing calls for a severe punishment.
Magistrate:	OK Mgweno Mhose do you have anything to say in mitigation?
Mgweno:	First, I have a wife, secondly I have children, then the farm and weeding time is close, then I have to attend CCM meetings.
Magistrate:	According to the law of the United Republic of Tanzania, article 110/220/1958 it is clear that you Mgweno are guilty of making a schoolgirl pregnant. Also that you are an elderly man. To deter men from impregnating schoolgirls you will go to prison for five years with hard labour.
Mgweno:	Oooooh noooo!
Magistrate:	You Asha, for allowing this old man to deceive you, for putting your schooling expenses to waste and to serve as a lesson to other girls, I am sentencing you to imprisonment for three months.
Asha:	(crying) No no no!
Mother:	No. Asha my daughter is going to jail, oh no!

The dance picks up the performance immediately by singing the last stanza of the song:

> Asha na Mgweno, wote mkafungwe
> Chitendo chomtendile, wote mkafungwe.
>
> *Translation:*
> Asha and Mgweno, both of you should go to jail
> For what you have done, both of you should go to jail.

The dancers continue dancing for a few minutes and then dance out to the same song which the audience has joined in singing.

The Chizalia group's performance dealt with the situation of the village accounts. Like the Bigililo show, it was a mixture of dance and dramatic skits as described below. The dancers enter with an introductory song singing the praises of the dance group and its leaders. They enter into the performing area with this song. Once at the centre, the group is divided into two groups and they start miming scenes at the village shop and at the village grain mill. Dialogue starts at the village shop:

Shop attendant:	There is no salt.
Villager:	Matches please.
Shop attendant:	The matches are finished.
Villager 2:	Sugar.
Shop attendant:	Nothing. It is finished.
Villager 3:	But how come! Didn't the sugar stock come only today?
Shop attendant:	It was a very small amount.
Villager 2:	These shops have bad practice.
Villager 3:	Sorry my friend.
Villager 4:	The things here are for the big people.
Shop attendant:	Put these things aside. They are for the elders. And those sacks there, put them away. Ooh! welcome elder. May I help you? Do you need sugar?
Village elder:	What is the price?
Shop attendant:	We have fixed the price ourselves.
Village elder:	I want to see the shop accounts. Why is your handwriting not steady?
Shop attendant:	Ooh, it is nothing.
Village elder:	What is inside here? I want to see.
Shop attendant:	No no it is nothing really.
Village elder:	Did the villagers see this?
Shop attendant:	No. Well I am not sure.
Village elder:	Do you think the villagers are fools? They see everything.
Shop attendant:	I had put one kilo aside for you.
Village elder:	No I don't want that. How much money did you realise today?

The skits is picked up by a song, a continuation of the same song but adding more words as follows:

> Tingo na nusu
> Rudi nyuma mbele basi
> Na mnapokea ngoma
> Miradi yetu Msoga

Tanzania motomoto
Tingo na nusu
Rudi nyuma mbele basi

Translation:
One step and a half
Go back and then forward and stop
and the drums pick up now
Our projects in Msoga
They excel in the whole of Tanzania
One step and a half
Go back and then forward and stop

A scene at a village meeting.

Chairman:	Up with CCM
Villagers:	Up! Up! Up!
Chairman:	OK. The meeting is declared open, welcome citizens. Are there any questions?
Villager 1:	I have a question, Comrade chairman. I am glad that today I came early. I have come to inquire about what you said the other day that the next meeting you call you shall give us the village accounts. Have you brought the accounts?
Chairman:	The task of preparing the accounts is very big. Since the day we promised we have been working on it but it is a difficult job.
Villagers:	(saying different things at the same time) You leaders are something else. You have eaten our money. What the hell is wrong with this village? Tomorrow, the day after. Since September they promised. Where are our accounts?

The dance picks up here with the song:

Wananchi wa Msoga
Tumechoka na siasa
Viongozi tunasema
Wananchi wa Msoga

Tumechoka na siasa
Tingo na nusu, rudi nuyma mbele basi.

Translation:
We Residents of Msoga
Are fed up with politics
We are telling you leaders
We Residents of Msoga are fed up with politics
One step and a half, go back and then forward and stop.

(The meeting continues)

Villager:	Now it is September, you must keep your promise.
Villager:	Yes, this is the month you promised.
Chairman:	Citizens, why are you so much in a hurry?
Villager:	Isn't this September?
Chairman:	There is a very small section left.
Villagers:	(a big row in the meeting) No no we won't accept that. We want it today. Today, yes, today.
Chairman:	Friends, let us not spoil our development. Up with Msoga!

(Villagers boo.) (The audience also joins the booing amidst a lot of laughter.)

The dance starts again and continues while there is a lot of discussion and laughter in the audience. Then the meeting continues.

Elder:	(to the chairman) Do not fool around, the villagers are very serious, they are angry.
Elder:	This is also the year for the elections, watch out, please.

(The song picks up here. It is sung as a solo with the rest coming in to sing the chorus at the end.)

Wana kijiji wa Msoga tunayo malalamiko
Kuhusu mahesabu ya pesa zetu za kijiji
Tukitaka kuyajua viongozi wanakwepa
Tingo na nusu, rudi nyuma mbele basi.

Wanakijiji wa Msoga nguvu zetu zalegea
Sisi wa Msoga mahesabu hatupati
Wageni mliokuja mjue tatizo letu
Huo ndio mwisho wa habari
Rudi nyuma nenda mbele, tingo na nusu.

Chorus:
Viongozi wa Msoga
Tupeni hesabu zetu
Wananchi wa Msoga
Tumechoka na siasa.

Translation:
We citizens of Msoga have complaints
About our village accounts.
When we ask about the accounts the village leaders avoid the issue.
One and a half step, go forward and stop.
We Msoga citizens are losing morale for work
We of Msoga are not getting our accounts.
You visitors who have come you should know our problem.
That is the end of the story.
Go back and forward, one and a half step.

Chorus:
You leaders of Msoga, give us our accounts.
We citizens of Msoga are fed up with politics.

The same format was followed for the skit on health by the same group. It was based on the negative attitudes of the medical personnel at the village dispensary. The song's content was: "If the services are not good, work cannot be done. We Tanzanians like development. People who are concerned with ill-treating us please reform." The story line shows the medical officer who does not even have the patience to listen to the patients. He uses foul language to the patients and dishes out medicine without even diagnosis. And he prescribes aspirin for every ailment. The song ends by pleading with the medical personnel to give good service to the people.

The story line of the Mkwajungoma group was based on the development tax and youth organisation. A very old woman is seen cleaning her house, a grandson enters and they chat about development tax after which he leaves. People's militia come and arrest the old woman for not paying her development tax and take her to court. Three youths appear chatting about development tax. They hear about the grandmother of one of them. They decide to contribute 40 shillings. They agree to start a farm out of which they will be able to solve their financial problems. After a while, though, one of them runs away to town looking for a job. But he is arrested under the human deployment campaign and is sent back to the village where he rejoins his friends at their farm.

Post-performance discussion

The discussion held immediately after the performances was chaired by an elderly villager. The discussion was geared towards evaluating the problems and trying to arrive at some solutions. There were heated arguments and wide participation from those present, both men and women. The following are the comments and suggestions advanced during the discussion.

On unwanted pregnancies:

(a) Parents should work hand in hand with the teachers. Both should exert a certain discipline over the schoolchildren, especially the girls.
(b) Sex education should be introduced in the schoolsystem and parents, teachers and doctors should participate in the exercise.
(c) The traditional initiation ceremony done for girls at puberty should be delayed until they finish primary school. This would ensure that their sex education is given at a time when they finish school, when they can more responsibly handle it. At present, many girls were undergoing the ceremony while still in primary school and are tempted to try out their knowledge.
(d) Teachers, some of whom were responsible for the pregnancies, should stop using student labour especially girls because this gives them a chance to lure the girls to their houses leading to sexual relations.
(e) Technical education should be offered after primary school or simultaneously with primary education. This would alle-

viate the unemployment problem among both boys and girls and it would also deter the girls from being lured by the incomes of the men.

On the village accounts:

(a) It was true that the village leadership had misappropriated the village funds. The village government colluded with the person who was reported to have broken into the village office and stolen the village money. This was so because the village government had not taken any serious step to apprehend the culprit. The fact that the leadership had failed to produce the accounts for four years meant that they had misused the money, or the leadership must be absolutely incompetent and ineffective. The village chairman must take responsibility for this state of affairs because he failed to force the treasurer to produce the statement of accounts.

(b) Whoever is responsible for the disappearance of the village funds must be apprehended.

(c) Legal action must be taken against the treasurer but first of all he must submit the accounts to the village.

(d) The village government must ensure that they check the accounts books regularly.

(e) The village chairman and his committee should either resign or pledge to work more diligently, otherwise the people would not be willing to work on the village development projects.

(f) The village chairman admitted to the shortcomings of his administration and pledged to rectify the situation and to follow up the accounts issue.

(g) A deadline was given of one month during which the treasurer was to produce the accounts. At the expiry of that period legal action would be taken. Legal action would also be taken depending on the situation of the accounts when submitted.

On the development tax:

(a) As stipulated in the national development tax law, the village should give the names of people who had no capacity for paying the tax either due to old age or absolute poverty.

(b) All people who can work should do so and pay the tax as stipulated. Many people cannot pay the tax because they do not want to engage in production.

On the youth:

(a) It was true that some youth were lazy and did not want to work on the land. Others work hard, but lack an organisation to guide them. The youth should form a body that will unite them and enable them to organise income generating activities.
(b) The youth of the Mkwajungoma group asked for a plot of land from the village saying that they were ready to start a youth farm project and they were asking the village to support them.

On the agricultural inputs the possibilities of securing the tractor were discussed. It was pointed out, however, that the morale of the people had gone low because of the leadership problems. If that was solved people could easily mobilise to get the agricultural inputs. They could even contribute money to a village tractor.

The problem of the negative attitudes of the medical personnel caused an angry outburst from one of the nurses at the village dispensary because she was not in agreement with the portrayal of the medical personnel in the play. There was much laughter in the audience, and one person asked her why she was so offended if she was not the culprit. It turned out that she was actually one of the most rude ones. The medical officer, the target of the play, also tried to explain his position but the people refused to accept his arguments.

Follow-up action

For follow-up it was agreed that similar workshops should be held in the future. Also that the youths' request be met since there was land in the village and that a follow-up be made of their project to ensure its success. The village accounts were to be submitted in one month's time at the latest and legal action taken against the culprits. It should be mentioned here that the animateurs did seek the assistance of the Legal Aid Committee based at the University of Dar es Salaam to assist the villagers on how to approach the legal aspect of their village funds. A committee was to be set up to draw up the list of those incapable of paying the development levy, and it was hoped that the message had reached home about the medical personnel and their behaviour.

CHAPTER 10
Mkambalani Popular Theatre Workshop 1986

In September 1986, a twelve day Popular Theatre workshop was conducted in Mkambalani village, 25 kilometres from Morogoro town in Eastern Tanzania. The workshop was organised and conducted by the team of animateurs from the University of Dar es Salaam who had conducted the other workshops discussed above, and was yet another attempt to continue the Popular Theatre practice. The animateurs set out to use their experiences from Malya, Bagamoyo, and Msoga to improve on the Popular Theatre process and to seek ways of overcoming the shortcomings of the previous workshops. Yet it was also to be a new experience because the team was to work with a new community with a different cultural background. The system of including both cultural workers from the Bagamoyo College of Art and the local cultural officers was also used in this workshop. The cultural officers were learning through participation how to organise and conduct Popular Theatre programmes. There were ten animateurs in total.[1]

Background to Mkambalani

Mkambalani is situated in the Morogoro Rural District. Although it is a village in its own right it has not been officially registered and is considered part of Kitungwa village. Everything concerning Mkambalani is, therefore, administered from Kitungwa and even though there is a village government in Mkambalani, it has little power to effect decisions without the consent of the leadership in

---

1. For more details on this workshop, see Lihamba, A. and P. Mlama 1986, *Ripoti warsha ya Sanaa kwa maendeleo ya jamii Msoga*, Chuo Kikuu Cha, (unpublished), Dar es Salaam; and Lihamba, A. and P. Mlama 1987, *Women and Communication: Popular Theatre as an Alternative Medium*, (unpublished), Association of African Women for Research on Development, Dakar.

power to effect decisions without the consent of the leadership in Kitungwa. This situation has contributed much to the political and economic problems of Mkambalani. The recent history of the village is one of struggle for a status of independence.

Mkambalani lies next to a huge sisal plantation and has served as a labour reserve for the plantation since the 1930s. Mkambalani itself, however, has plenty of land because the soil of the area on which Mkambalani is placed was considered unsuitable for sisal. Not much was invested in the Mkambalani area by the colonial government which was only interested in the sisal estates. For example, social service like water and health centres were only provided at the sisal estates for the workers and not for the surrounding villages like Mkambalani.

During the villagisation programme in 1974, Mkambalani village was abolished and the inhabitants ordered to move to a nearby village. It was soon discovered, though, that Mkambalani village was abolished by mistake because it was not on the official list of abolished villages. It was also known that the removal was the result of the machinations of some leaders in the district. This started a long struggle with the system to get Mkambalani recognised as a village.

First, the people decided to confront the officials and demand the right to move back to their original village which they did in 1976. In 1977 official approval was given to have the village surveyed in preparation for its official status as a village. But some officials in the district were displeased with these developments. An order was given by the District Commissioner for the villagers to move, and a people's militia was even sent to evict the villagers who refused to move. The villagers resisted this eviction and decided to send a delegation to the Prime Minister in 1978. Two more delegations were sent in 1981 and 1983. An official delegation from the Prime Minister came to the village, and it decided that the village should remain; but while waiting for the official registration process to be completed they should choose one of the neighbouring villages as their official representative. They choose Kitungwa. However, because the registration process has to go through the district offices, it has been delayed until now and the village was still not recognised officially as a village.

The population of Mkambalani is 1,500 and like many villages in Tanzania, agricultural production is the main economic activity. Cotton is the major cash crop and food crops include maize, beans, cassava, and bananas. Agriculture is on a subsistence level. Because of its closeness to Morogoro town, people also engage in petty business and both men and women often work as casual labourers in the sisal plantations. Beer brewing is another source of income, especially for women.

Because of its non-official status, Mkambalani has no school, no health centre or any of the other services which are normal for villages. They have to depend on the neighbouring villages. The village also has an acute problem of inadequate water supply. There are water taps which were part of a project by the Netherlands government for Morogoro region but the taps are dry most of the year. The water supply at the traditional open wells also dwindles during the dry season. The villagers and especially the women have to walk long distances in search of water.

Research and problem analysis

Prior to the workshop, the two workshop co-ordinators had visited the village and made the necessary official contacts at the regional and district levels. Even though the team was not completely new to the village, the first two days were spent getting to know it. On the first day the team met the village elders including the village chairman and his secretary.

On the morning of the second day there was also a meeting with the village council and other elders to discuss the programme for the workshop. It was the intention of the animateurs to go straight into the research stage of the workshop on that day. The villagers, however, had planned this day as an official opening of the workshop to be presided over by the District Commissioner. Prior attempts to discourage them from such officialdom had not succeeded because the villagers felt that the occasion would draw official attention to the village where the district and regional officials were rarely seen. Moreover, the villagers wanted to read a message to the District Commissioner expressing their view of the various problems they were facing. They thought inviting him to the workshop was the only way they could get him to come and listen to them. In preparation for the official welcome the villagers had, on a voluntary basis, cleared and decorated a large area in front of the Party office. This entailed cutting down trees, rehabilitating the road leading to the area, clearing the bush in the surrounding areas and building some shelters to accommodate the visitors and those attending the ceremony. Arrangements were also made for food and drink for the guest of honour and his entourage at the village's expense.

The opening was scheduled for the afternoon. Four village dance groups were performing and most of the villagers gathered for the ceremony. All other activities were officially closed including drinking places. The District Commissioner, however, did not turn up even though he had agreed to come. The opening was scheduled for 3.00 pm, but it was not until 6.30 that a messenger came with the news that the District Commissioner could not come because of other official business and that he would instead come on the following day. There was, obviously, much disappointment over this, but the villagers decided that they would return for the opening the following afternoon. Meanwhile, the dance groups decided to continue dancing until well past midnight. The team of animateurs took this opportunity to dance with the villagers to familiarise themselves with the dances and get to know the people better. The following day people gathered again for the opening with the dance groups in attendance, but again the District Commissioner did not come. The villagers were very bitter especially over the flimsy reason given that he had no transport because his official car was in the garage for repairs. The following morning the villagers saw the same car passing by their village coming from Dar es Salaam and going to Morogoro.

The animateurs had used the waiting time to research into the problems of the village. Observing the cotton selling session carried out by the cotton authority revealed that the cotton authority officials were cheating the villagers by reducing the number of kilos during the weighing process. This was conducted in such a way that the farmer had no chance of reading the scale because after putting his cotton on the scale he was required to move immediately to the cashier.

Further research also revealed many other irregularities. The cotton authorities harassed the villagers by threatening to refuse to buy their cotton unless they provided the weighing scales and storage facilities for the cotton. Even though it is the duty of the cotton authorities to provide both the scales and storage, the Mkambalani villagers had to provide both on this particular day. It was possible, however, with the intervention of the animateurs, to stop the cheating and to make the cotton officials repeat the weighing of all the cotton and pay the villagers according to the proper weight of their produce. Many villagers found that they had been cheated by up to eight kilos during the previous weighing and were happy to get their money.

The research picked up momentum on the following day. Together with the members of the village the animateurs made a tour of the whole area of the village seeing the different activities and talking to the villagers about various issues. Because the village area was very big and the villagers were determined to show the team the whole area, more time was spent walking around than of talking with the villagers. Therefore it was decided that more information be sought for throughout the workshop and more effort be directed making contact with people whenever possible. The major problems were identified as the following:

(a) *Registration of the village.* Because the village had no official recognition, it was difficult to plan and implement development programmes. The village also seemed to have reached a stalemate in terms of what to do next because all their previous efforts had not produced expected results. At the appropriate government offices they were given reasons for their non-registration which to them had become a vicious circle.

(b) *Water supply.* The village is not getting water from the taps most of the year. The traditional open wells also dry up during the dry season. A modern well sunk by the Lions Club as a donation to the village is also out of order.

(c) *Problems connected with agricultural activities.* Expansion of agriculture has been difficult because of the unavailability of tractors and agricultural inputs such as seeds, insecticides, machine batteries, for spraying crops such as cotton, and fertilizers. The villagers are also discouraged from growing cash crops because often these are not bought by the authorities. Crops stay in the homes for long periods because the authorities claim that they do not have the money to purchase them. In fact at the time of the workshop most of the cotton had not yet been bought and the simsim and sunflower of the previous season were rotting in people's houses. The villagers also reported that the reluctance to work on the village's communal farm was because the original farm which they had cleared and planted had been taken away by the then District Commissioner and given to two private individuals from the town.

(d) *Lack of essential services*. The village does not have a school or a dispensary and depends on the neighbouring villages for such services. The educational performance of the children of the village is not good because not only do they have to walk long distances but often they have to stay hungry for most of the day. Some children opt not to go to school at all. The dependency on the neighbouring village for medical services has also proved a strain on the dispensary whose drug allocation is based on the number of residents of its own village only. There is therefore a constant shortage of drugs even though the medical personnel is willing to help.

An analysis of the village registration problem brought up the following viewpoints:

(1) The officials do not want Mkambalani registered and therefore deliberately delay the process. The villagers believed that the leaders at all levels, that is, the ward, division and district level were colluding to make sure that the village is not registered. This was due to a long conflict between the village and the leaders. The leaders' original motive for abolishing the Mkambalani village was said to have been their interest in establishing private farms in the area. In fact a number of leaders already had private farms in the village.

(2) The Kitungwa village leadership which for the time being was responsible for the administration of Mkambalani had joined the other leaders in suppressing the registration of Mkambalani because Kitungwa would loose its strength as a village because most of the developmental work was con-

ducted in Mkambalani, and Mkambalani left on its own would be a stronger village than Kitungwa.

(3) The official reason given for not registering Mkambalani included the argument that the village did not have enough land area to be a village. But the irony of it was that the "big" people who claimed this were themselves farm owners or are asking for land in the village. Research revealed that 57 acres of land in the village was owned by the officials from Morogoro town, including the Regional Development directors, the Regional Commissioner, an army officer, two top engineers, a marketing manager at the shoe company, and the Director of the Government Stores. The question then asked was: If Mkambalani was too small where did these people get their farms from?

(4) As to why the villagers allowed or gave their land to the officials it was explained that the villagers thought that if the leaders themselves were members of the village by having farms it would hasten the process of the registration.

(5) The other official reason for non-registration was that Mkambalani did not have development projects to show that it could be a good village. This was countered by the argument that in fact Mkambalani produces more agricultural crops than the neighbouring villages which have been registered after their application. They have also built through self-help a Party office as well as the village shop. A question was also asked as to what came first, development projects or the registration of the village. It was pointed out that as long as they are not registered they cannot be considered for bank loans, schools, health centres and so on.

The animateurs took the effort to go and see the leaders at the ward, and division district level to get the official position on the registration issue. During the interviews the unfavourable attitude towards Mkambalani was apparent. It was said that the Mkambalani people were very stubborn and had no development spirit. Official records, though, revealed that the application for the registration of Mkambalani which had been tendered on May 26th 1981 had received no feedback from the District level where it was still lying. A query from the Regional Commissioner of September

25th 1985 as to why Mkambalani had not been registered received a reply from the district that there was a boarder dispute between Mkambalani and one of the neighbouring villages, Fulwe. It is true that there was such a boarder dispute but the villagers believe it is all part of the conflict with the leaders. There was also a bureaucratic reason given to the Regional Commissioner in that the responsibility of registering villages had been shifted from the old department of Registrar of Co-operatives to that of the Registrar of Ujamaa villages, and no registrations could take place because the registrar had not yet been appointed. None of these reasons had ever been communicated to the villagers.

The water problem was affecting the village very seriously. People, especially the women, had to walk at least six kilometres to the next water source as a result of which both their health and agricultural production were affected. If they opted to get water at the traditional wells in the village they had to spend long hours in the queues because the water was coming out in mere trickles. A lot of animosity had arisen out of fights for places in the morning queue. There have been accusations of witchcraft due to the quarrels at the well. There is also ill feeling against the richer families who can buy water and take most of the water from the wells for brewing beer for sale.

The villagers believed that their water problem is tied up with the registration issue. They believed that the officials took no step to solve the water problem in order to make them so frustrated that they would leave the village, and then the officials would get the land they were after. The District water engineer, visited during the workshop for an official explanation to the problem, pointed out that there were broken old water pipes that needed replacement and that the district did not have the funds. Also the drying up of the water taps was, according to him, due to the decrease in water pressure caused by the increase in population in the area.

The villagers refuted the broken tap argument from the District water engineer. They reported that they had themselves checked the whole tap system and there was no evidence of a broken tap anywhere along the line. It was also pointed out that if the pressure was low how come the District engineer had authorised the diversion of the water meant for Mkambalani village to three individual farmers who were now watering their banana farms day and night while the villagers were going without water. Even though the issue of the diversion of the water to these private farmers had been taken up at the ward development committee meeting no effective step had been taken.

As to the problems connected with agricultural activities, the ward agricultural officer was of the opinion that the villagers did not engage in agricultural activities because of laziness and that they preferred to engage in petty business because it was physically less taxing. The villagers, however, insisted that their problems were the ones stated above. It was also later discovered that the ward agricultural officer was very unpopular. The villagers found her both rude and uninterested in their problems.

On the question of essential services the villagers believed that if their village was registered they would be able to acquire the essential services like a school or a dispensary. They were aware of the fact that acquiring the services in terms of structures would not necessarily provide the goods. They brought up the problems they were facing with the shop which they had built themselves. Commodities were not adequate. Also the distribution system at the ward level encouraged embezzlement, unfairness, and irresponsibility. In the whole period of January to September, for instance, the village shop had only been allocated 100 kilogrammes of sugar for its 1,500 people. The distribution in the village of the little that was available was also unjust.

The theatre process

The problems discussed above were researched and explored during discussions inside and outside the village, in formal and informal gatherings. It was the performances, however, which potently expressed these problems and the way they were perceived by the villagers. Unlike the meetings where participation was limited to a few village elders, all of them men, everyone participated in the performances. In the performances the people showed both spontaneity and a frankness which had not been possible during the previous meetings and discussions. Some issues came out only during the performances. The villagers touched the issues either directly of indirectly, symbolically or metaphorically. The choice was dictated by the nature of the forms as well as the thematic content of the problems under discussion.

Each day of the workshop was usually divided into three parts. Most villagers attended to their various activities in the mornings. The guest participants, the village elders and a few others met in small groups for discussion or engaged in the research needed for that day. Except for the youth group which met in the morning, the performing groups met individually in the afternoon to discuss issues arising from their theme and to give them artistic expression. The day ended with all groups performing in the village square. During the last days of the workshop, the performances were followed by discussions with the members of the community present to evaluate the day's activities, the performances and the problems expressed. The way each group worked and used its form for the particular problem it was dealing with can best be shown by looking at each group in turn.

Gombesugu

This group looked at the issue of the village registration as their main theme but the problems in the village are so intertwined that there was, often, an overflow from one problem to another during the performances.

Gombesugu is a celebratory dance performed during such events as weddings, or initiation ceremonies. Its essential instruments are *manyanga* and *sugu*. There are usually two groups of lead singers with two people in each and everyone present acts as chorus. The dance format and songs are close to *Nzekule* (see below) but while both use *manyanga*, there is no *sugu* in *Nzekule*.

While the leader of this group was a man, the lead singers were both women and men who had worked together making up the songs. At any particular time during the workshop, the core participants in this group ranged from four to fifteen, getting larger as the workshop progressed. The age range in the group was between 30 and 60, and they would perform anywhere when invited. The group had no formal organization, but they nevertheless acted as a unit.

The group already had a wide repertoire of songs which praise, lament, teach, celebrate, and criticise political and social issues. So besides creating songs specifically about the problem of the registration of the village, the group had already a repertoire of songs on this and other issues of the village. The following is an example of this group's performance—first of all the group danced to the following song:

Maneno yako sema	Speak the words
Usiogope sema	Don't be afraid speak
Maji hatuna	We have no water
Hospitali hatuna	We don't have a hospital
Shule hatuna	We don't have a school
Wazo la pili tunasema	As a second thought we say
Tumekuwa jela Mkambalani	We are imprisoned in Mkambalani
Tumechoka	We are tired
Kama kijiji hakitakiwi tuelezwe	If the village is not wanted tell us
Yatoke uwanjani hapo	Let it be said in public then
Maneno yako sema	Speak the words
Usiogope sema	Don't be afraid speak

The song was sung half way through, then a recitation of the history of the village was performed, after which the song was resumed until the end. There followed a short scenario where two people entered the circle and sat down. A third person approached them and demanded why they did not want to join the village. The two in the centre remained silent. The third man tried to pull them out by force but the two did not budge. Then slowly, they started a second song which was a lament for the village and its inhabitants:

Mwenyewe najua	I deeply know
Mnanitesa	you are oppressing me
Mamie mwali	woman
Wananitesa	they are oppressing me
Kijiji Mkambalani	Mkambalani village
Wana Fitina	they have a conspiracy
Mwana kolila	the child is crying
Mama wa mwali	woman
Mkambalani	Mkambalani
Wananitafuta	They are against it

Mnanitesa	your are oppressing me
Sipati shule	I can't get school
Maji sipati	Water I can't get
Wananitesa	They are oppressing me
Mkambalani	Mkambalani
Koki wanaiba	They steal the corks
Maji hatuna	We have no water
Mnanicheka	you laugh at me
Wengine wakipenda kijiji	Others love the village
Hatutoki hapa	We are not moving
Wanasema mpaka wafe	They say until they die
Mwenyewe najua	I deeply know

The order of the songs and the words were not strictly adhered to. During several performances, the first song came second while the verses did not always follow the same order. The content and the specific moods for each song as well as the myths, however, remained the same. In the second song cited above there is a typical free movement and association of ideas and emotions. It becomes not only a lament, but a strong protest against elements not supportive of the village. It calls for understanding from others who are oppressed, it provides a point of self-criticism (they steal corks) and expresses defiance. The song approaches the subject directly but the disjointed nature of the thought progression leaves much room for the listener and participant to fill in the missing links with her/his imagination. These elements which are inherent in the form from its traditional sources make it flexible and adaptable to a variety of themes and intentions.

Nzekule

The dance *Nzekule,* is closely associated with the initiation ceremonies known as *Mkole*. *Mkole* is the traditional rite of passage from girlhood to womanhood. It aims at inculcating into the initiate her new duties and responsibilities as an adult female member of the community, and the ceremonies and rituals take several days.

Mkole is usually an all women affair and only women who have themselves gone through the ceremony are allowed to participate in the initiation parts f the rituals. While the song accompanying *Mkole* dances are meant to teach the initiate aspects of her new status, the teaching is not always direct. There is much use of symbolic and metaphorical language, but this is always translated and directly related to the issues relevant to the initiate. There is a sharpness, however, in the language which is used to castigate evil and unsocial elements, laugh at human foibles, underline desirable values and instil general social responsibility. Topical issues, therefore, are easy to incorporate in the texts because they provide ready material for the songs which are either improvised on the spot or prepared in advance. It is not uncommon to see individuals and groups on the opposite side of an issue using the songs to communicate their views to each other, to put each other down or to protest. *Nzekule* carries all these characteristics of *Mkole* dances and songs.

As pointed out above, *Nzekule* is a dance which is closely related to *Gombesugu* and in the village one group usually performs both dances. *Nzekule*, however, is a dance dominated by women, and this was the most dynamic group during the workshop performances. The women who ranged from the young to the old used the dance to express themselves on a variety of issues but especially the scarcity of water in the village. From the first day of the workshop, the women improvised and spontaneously created songs relevant to the issue but they also drew upon a reservoir of old songs. The women who usually sat quiet at meetings and listened to the men expressed their anger, frustration, helplessness, and protest through the songs. While some songs were rehearsed in the group before performance, many more were improvised on the spot during performance. The following is a representative sample of the group's songs:

Mkambalani mateso (chorus)	There is a suffering in Mkambalani
Kijiji kina kilema hiki	This village is disabled
Hakina maji	It has no water
Kijiji tunakipenda	We love the village
Lakini kina kilema	But it is disabled
Tunalia eehe	We cry eehe
Mwaka huu sikulima	I have not farmed this year
Tutalima saa ngapi	When can we farm

Wakubwa mmetuchoka	You are tired of us you big ones
Mnatuona wachafu	You see us dirty
Nguo kufua hatufui	We do not wash our clothes
Wala kuoga hatuogi	Nor do we bathe
Wakubwa mnatucheka	You laugh at us you big ones
Wenzetu nyie wasafi	You are clean
Wenzetu nyie wasafi	You are clean
Wenzenu tunanuka	We smell
Kijiji tunakitaka	We want the village
Lakini tunashindwa	But we are losing
Wakubwa wametuchoka	The big ones are tired of us
Wanataka tukihame	They want us to move away
Lakini tunasema hatuhami	But we say we shall not move away

While the women did spend time each day discussing the issue of water, they preferred to express themselves through the songs and would begin a song whenever they felt deeply about an issue which was currently under discussion. For example, a very sensitive issue concerning the village was introduced in the workshop in this way. Up to that point, no one had talked about the issue in any of the discussions.

One day in the middle of discussing the water problem, two women stood up and started a song:

> Duka la kijiji lina lawama
> Sukari vitenge kwa wanachama
> Kibiriti sigara kali mali ya wanyonge

Translation:
> The village shop carries a blame
> Sugar *vitenge* go to (party) members
> Matches cheap cigarettes are for the poor

This song was referring to the unfair practice of the village leadership to let coveted and essential commodities be sold to party members while the others were only allowed to buy less desirable goods. The song was enthusiastically picked up by the rest of the women present who danced and provided the chorus. The two song leaders then led the whole group to where the village chairman and his committee was sitting. After singing for a while they improvised the following scenario:

A: I want one kilo of sugar.
B: What sugar, show the card (party card)!
C: I have none.
B: You have no card? Go (sharply), get out!
C: Those with cards only get sugar and *vitenge*.
D: If you have no card, get out!
B: (Speaks quitely to someone behind) Wait for me. You want sugar—go behind and wait for me.

The song and dance were repeated. Khadija (lead singer/dancer): *Vitenge*, sugar to those with cards. Now a drum call has gone out that *manyanga* (i.e. performers) are needed at the CCM office. There are guests, there is a workshop. Khadija should go and play *manyanga*. Now we have been playing *manyanga* since the day before yesterday. So, why wasn't I Khadija asked my card to play *manyanga*? How come I was not asked Khadija, do you have your card?

All: (ululate) yes, break open the gourd (say it).
Khadija: It is the fourth day today that we have played the *manyanga*, those with cards, are they here, are they not here?
All: Not here.

The song continued after this with everyone inserting their own comments on the issue. There was a prevailing sense of relief that this issue which had been preying on many minds, but had not come out in public discussion, was finally exposed. Everyone wanted to say something and complained about the discriminatory practice which provided a loophole for corruption. After this, the issue was discussed and an agreement reached that henceforth the village shop would not discriminate village members even if they were not party members. Apparently, the village government had been pressurised by the district party leadership to introduce the practice in order to encourage people to join the party. This incident shows how popular forms of expression release in people the power to speak more freely than they would have in other circumstances.

Kipuku

Kipuku like *Nzekule* is closely associated with initiation ceremonies. *Kipuku* has been traditionally used during the initiation of boys. When a boy reached puberty he was kept indoors until he was ready to come out. He was taken to the bush to be initiated into manhood and when he was returned to the village, *Kipuku* was danced. The songs in *Kipuku* are like those in *Nzekule* and *Gombesugu* in that they have a social function.

It was interesting to note, however, that whereas the two groups using *Nzekule* and *Gombesugu* sang most of their songs in Kiswahili with a little bit of the local language Kiluguru here and there, *Kipuku* was sung in Kiluguru only. Not only that, but the songs were never direct but made allusions to things and events or forced the imagination to substitute one thing for the other. Some kind of translation of the meaning of the song was always carried out to clarify its intention. The fact that *Kipuku* is usually favoured by the elders of the community can be one reason why the transition to Kiswahili has not taken place.

While the dance was open for all to participate in, the core group during the workshop was all men. Unlike the women in the *Nzekule* group, the elders in *Kipuku* preferred to discuss issues at length before they broke into a dance or song. Most of these elders have been in some village leadership position at one time or another and so easily lapsed into issues connected with the history of the village. Most of the elders participating in this group were great narrators and so besides the *Kipuku* dance, many stories were told to illustrate, underline or raise some issues. For the most part, the problems connected with agricultural activities which the group had to deal with was not specifically underlined in either the *Kipuku* songs or the narrated stories. The elders were deeply affected by the oppression and exploitation which they saw as Mkambalani's lot. The songs lamented and protested about the arrogance of the leaders who looked down on them, ignored them or simply wanted to get rid of them. As in the performances of the other groups, the songs and the stories displayed their defiance and optimism to overcome the problems they faced. The following are two representative songs and a story by this group:

Simba wamkomile lukonde
Mgulu mumu mgulu simba
Mwee iwakulu wamkanganya

Translation:
The lion that was killed in Lukonde
was discovered to be half lion half man
O! we are in trouble from the big people

The song referred to the coming of the colonial master whom the Africans thought was a good man only to realise later that he was an animal. Likewise the "big people" pretend to be good, but in fact they are lions preying on the people.

Mbee vipala	Young men
Mvale tuluki mwee	dress up for war
lekela dingila mbee	Don't let the enemy invade,
mvale mwale tuluki	dress up for war

The elders explained that the song was a call to war because the "big people" have invaded the village. It calls for the youth to be ready to fight them.

Hadithi ya Kichwa Upande (The story of the one with the lop-sided head)
There was once a sultan who had seven children. The eldest was very ugly because his head was misshapen and lop-sided and he was therefore known as Kichwa upande. His brothers hated him. One day, the brothers decided to travel to a far away land but they did not want *Kichwa upande* to come with them. The latter was very cunning, however, and followed them. When they found out the other brothers were very angry. They eventually arrived in the land ruled by an evil sultan who plotted to kill the brothers. *Kichwa upande*, however, discovered the sultan's intentions and substituted the sultan's own children for his brothers. So it came to pass that unknowingly the sultan killed his own children while *Kichwa upande* and his brothers escaped. The brothers showered much praise and gratitude on *Kichwa upande* for his courage and wisdom.

The elders felt that the leaders like the brothers of *Kichwa upande* looked down on them because they were poor. In reality, however, it is they, the poor peasants, who are the backbone of development in the country.

Mkwajungoma (Zembwela group)

Mkwajungoma is a dance which is originally from the Wazaramo people but like many traditional dances in the country it has become popular in many places. The dance is very popular in the village, especially through the performances of the super Zembwela group which derives its name from a dancing style popularised by the Marquis du Zaire group, a famous band in the country. The Kizaramo word (kuzembwela) means walking-slowly-with-much-body-talk.

This group was made entirely of the village youths, both boys and girls and it was the only group which had rules and regulations about membership. They had a membership fee (T.Sh. 50) and the group accepted invitations to perform for a small fee during various functions in the village and in the neighbouring villages. Out of the group of 22 members only 4 were girls. This is primarily because the village girls have more responsibilities at home than the boys. Moreover, it is difficult for the girls to commit themselves to go outside the village because most parents are reluctant to let their girls travel far from home without supervision. The group also excludes those who have not finished their primary education or reached puberty.

The group performs *Mkwajungoma* according to choreographic formations which they create according to the rules of the dance. They have a leader who organises the steps and leads the group in the dancing and singing. Besides performing *Mkwajungoma*, this group created several scenarios to depict the problems of lack of social services such as a school and a hospital. Unlike the other groups whose time was limited because of other responsibilities, this group spent most days of the workshop discussing, rehearsing, and creating new songs and scenarios. Their performances depicted not only the problems of lack of social services but they also incorporated other problems of the village such as lack of water and the oppression that leaders at various levels are exercising upon them.

The group tended also to bring into discussion and the performances national topical issues which the other groups did not pay much attention to. For example, one of the national topical issues at the time of the workshop was President Ali Hassan Mwinyi's call for leadership accountability which resulted in him being given an iron broom by Dar es Salaam Region to symbolise the task of sweeping corruptive and ineffective leadership from the nation's places of work. During the workshop, the youth group composed some scenarios which incorporated this issue, but put it in the context of Mkambalani thus underlining the need to uproot some ineffective leaders in the village. It is interesting to note that it was the women's group, *Nzekule* and this youth group, Zembwela, which brought up issues that pointed a finger at problems of leadership within the village. Both used the performances rather than the discussions as their medium to express their frustration and protest against some of their leaders whom they saw as part of Mkambalani's problems.

The following is a short summary of one of the short plays and a song created by this group on the hospital issue. Three people aroused each other early to go to their farms. On the way they discuss problems in their village e.g. lack of water, schools etc. While digging on the farm, one of them is bitten by a snake. The other two together with a relative of the sick man decide to take him to a hospital. It takes them eight hours to get there because of the distance and lack of transport. This skit was supposed to underline the need for accessible health facilities. There were songs before and after the performance of the above on the same issue.

Viongozi tuwe Imara

Viongozi msiyumbe yumbe x 2
Wananchi wataka bender
Wananchi wataka maji
Matatizo yamejitokeza
Kama vile maji hayatoki
Yanazuiliwa na wale mabepari
Wanamwagilia mashambani mwao
Viongozi mwogopane
Kuwakosa viongozi wazembe

Fagio la chuma liwafuatilie
Vijana wenu tuko imara.

Leaders must be firm
Don't sway leaders x 2
People want the flag
People want water
the problems which stand out
are like lack of water
Those capitalists are blocking the water
They are irrigating their farm
Leaders don't fear each other
To criticise
The iron broom should follow them
We the youth are firm.

Both the songs and the skits of the youth group tended to be less poetic and metaphorical but like many cultural groups in the country which have been exposed to ways of expressions encouraged by political leaders, they incorporated topical slogans and forms of parroting. They saw themselves as not only a cultural troupe but also as an organised unit who could carry out economic activities.

The village leadership tried to give encouragement to this group, and two related incidents during the workshop confirmed this. Because of the workshop and the expected coming of officials, the group was given uniforms to use during their performances. Moreover, arrangements were made to provide this group with food during the workshop. Both these examples created some friction between the other groups and the village leadership which was accused of favouritism. The issues were cleared after much discussion between the groups. Besides favouritism which these incidents displayed, they can also be seen as attempts by the village leadership to satisfy to some degree demands which such organised cultural groups as super Zembwela make i.e. the demand to have some of the basic needs of performers met by the community. It was agreed that the village would undertake to feed all those performers especially the leaders of the core groups who were spending much time attending to workshop activities.

All four groups had open rehearsals and invited the public to participate. Even though it was the artists of the core groups who were in charge of shaping the artistic pieces, the other members of the community joined the performances at will. In fact in Mkambalani, more than in the Malya or Msoga workshops, the public rehearsals were almost everyday performances with wide participation of the villagers. The *Nzekule* group, for instance, was creating new pieces every day, carried away by their emotions about their problems, especially the water problem and that of the village registration. It was very difficult for the animateurs to guide the performance into a deeper reflection of the issues involved and a sharper portrayal of the contradictions because the participation was almost too much. As was the case with Msoga, the villagers were their own masters of the artistic expressions and the animateurs were novices. It was also difficult to penetrate the artistic structure and to force sufficient change in form and content to radically address the issues involved. The people were so emotionally involved with the problems that they did not have much patience to stop dancing and discuss or analyse each aspect. They were more out to vent their anger and bitterness against what they considered as gross injustice to their village.

On the other hand, it was not necessary to change the artistic structure because all the dances had a flexible form that accommodated spontaneous creativity, addition of new content and the participation of whoever felt like being a part of the show. This is a characteristic of many African indigenous theatre forms. The Mkambalani workshop, more than the previous ones showed the great potential these theatre forms carry for use in Popular Theatre. Only time is needed to find a way to effectively integrate the objectives of Popular Theatre into the old artistic structures.

The final performance attracted about seven hundred people, of all sexes and age groups. It should be noted here that there were just as many people on the previous days for the rehearsals-cum-performances. The three groups presented pieces chosen from their repertoire of the previous days including those described earlier.

Post-performance discussion with the audience

The performance was followed immediately by a discussion with the audience in order to seek solutions to the problems. A member of the village chaired the discussion. The following are some quotations from what was said in the discussion (author's translation):

1. "You will see the leaders of the ward or division coming. Friends, we have these leaders. They want some land to farm. Land is given to them. We do that thinking that we are contributing to development only to find out that they are instead planning to abolish this village. They are turning this village into their own farm. I agree that we have the land. It is not true that we don't have land."
2. "They (the leaders) say that there isn't enough land but they come to ask for land. They are playing dirty games because we are poor. Since our young people (the animateurs) are here we ask them to listen carefully to our problems. About land we have it, we have Party cards whose subscriptions are fully paid and the population is enough (for registration). Those are our views."
3. "All the qualifications for village registration are there. If I heard right, there are murmurings that we have no development, that is why we are not a (registered) village. I am asking this question: who is responsible for development of people?"
4. "There was a surveyor staying there in Legeza Mwendo. He surveyed here, left, right, left, right, four streets. Today this is not a village, that surveyor who was surveying this village, where did he get his salary from? We are being oppressed but about our oppression, only God the Almighty knows."
5. "It is true that this village is now wanted because all the qualifications are there. Even I am surprised. I don't know what office sent the surveyors to come and survey the village and then refuse the village. That hatred for the village, did you find out at what level it starts at the offices you went to?"
6. "It is rumoured that we, the people of Mkambalani, do not obey orders from above. The hatred originated from the border conflict. The Division secretary, the Ward secretary and

the Councillor to whom we gave our votes made us sit down to determine the borders.

Some dirty talk has passed at the Ward, Division, District and Regional level. They were not happy that this village should be a village or even, as we do now, host this workshop (big audience applause). Today, because this workshop has come to us they are surprised, the baby has been given a turban to wear, there is evil talk. Our neighbours who have got the registration already depend on neighbouring hospitals and schools just like we do. To get registration a school is necessary. Pangawe has a school, but it was built by the colonial rulers. This is the tenth year since we started, but we are poor people, therefore we are driven around like the millipede because it has no eyes (big applause). Now we are asking everybody here to think about how we can get our own flag (villages normally fly the Party flag) and a registration number."

7. "The workshop and the village together should send a letter to the Regional Commissioner to get the proper information."
8. "The leaders are the ones who are oppressing us. We shall stand shoulder to shoulder, us and our visitors, we have to solve our problems. Let us together go and see what happens at the higher level. Let us go and find out whether we can stay in the village or whether we have to leave like in the beginning when they evicted us."
9. "Which level should we go to?"
10. "Because here at the bottom they are fed up with us, let us go to the region, to the Regional Commissioner himself."
11. "On the water problem it is the pipes to the plantations that are creating trouble for us, especially during the dry season. Those taps should be closed immediately to save people from suffering."
12. "What is the district doing to solve this problem?"
13. "About our struggles with the water problem, I have no faith in the young men who are servicing the water system for the villages. Our wives suffer. The water technician is Mshomari's (District water engineer) son-in-law. He does not even know how to hold a spanner, but he is Mshomari's son-in-

law and would Mshomari say no to his daughter? He does not clean the tank but waits until another technician comes to do it. The villagers should sit down and take all of this to court."
14. "The action needed is to get rid of this technician and put instead a child of this village who can feel for the village."
15. "The big problem is the three corks (pipe connections at the three plantations). Even if we employ a child of the village we won't get the water. Letters should be written to the leaders asking them to remove those three corks."
16. "If they could distribute the water equally by closing the taps to certain areas in turns, we could all get the water."
17. "The very leaders are involved in installing those pipes. They (the owners of the plantations) pay money to the leaders and pipes are fixed for them."
18. "Let us go to the region to ask who put in those corks; is the value of a banana tree the same as that of a human being?"
19. "Both issues together with the village registration should be taken to the region."
20. "We men don't sleep, our women sleep at the well, in the morning we go to the farms alone, the women have no time for any other work apart from getting water."

The discussion lasted two and a half hours and went right into the night. It had to be stopped because it was dark and people had to walk some distance to their homes.

Follow-up action

By the end of the discussion several suggestions had been given on how to solve the problems. There were two major follow-up plans which were agreed upon and specific concrete actions identified. These can be categorised as short term community action and long term action requiring further research with the involvement of outside assistance. The short term action included the following proposals which the villagers themselves could act upon:

(a) To alleviate the lack of water, the village will rehabilitate neglected traditional wells to make them produce more water. This will mean ensuring that the wells have the desired depth, are well protected and kept in good conditions. The villagers will also contribute money and buy new taps to replace the missing ones on the water pipes to avoid water wastage should the water be made available again. Mkambalani will also liaise with their neighbours who share the same water system to see if each village can have access to the available water in turns. A closer supervision of the water service man was also agreed upon.

(b) To stop the "big" people from expropriating village land it was decided that the village leadership should refuse to give such people land in the village.
(c) To ensure that the villagers are not cheated and get a fair price for their crops, especially cotton, the village decided to closely supervise all buying and selling of crops in the village.
(d) The village was to devise a fairer system of distributing essential commodities from the village shop.
(e) The village was to devise activities for the youth so that they could be self-reliant.

The long term action plans included the forming of a committee consisting of the villagers and the animateurs for the workshop which would be delegated to seek further information and clarification on the issues from the Morogoro Regional Commissioner. A committee of six was appointed and requested to ensure that the report on the workshop was written quickly, after which the village would write a letter to the Regional Commissioner in which the report would be enclosed, and then a delegation would be sent to seek an audience with the Regional Commissioner. The delegation consisted of the committee.

The workshop report was submitted by the village to the Regional Commissioner with copies to the District Commissioner, The District Party Chairman, the District Development Director and the District Water Engineer. The Regional Commissioner promised to call a meeting with the village committee once he and the regional and district officials had gone through the report. Before the meeting was called though, the Regional Commissioner was transferred. The one who replaced him could not attend to the Mkambalani problems until he had completed his familiarisation programme. The village kept going to the Regional offices to follow up on the issue.

In June 1988 the village was informed that permission had been granted by the authorities for the village to be registered. The village could go ahead with the preparations for getting the certificate and the official handing over of the certificate to the village. A visit to the village in August 1988 confirmed that these preparations were under way. The water taps had also started flowing again. On top of that a mobile health unit has been established in the village by the district, two youths from the village have been selected to train as rural medical aides in preparation for the setting up of a village dispensary.

Assistance had also been provided for a group of youth to train in handicrafts after which some of them have now started making mats and wall decorations. The villagers were also given assistance in acquiring building materials, especially corrugated iron roofing for which transport was provided from Morogoro town to the village.

The villagers are overjoyed by these developments, especially the village registration for which they have struggled for about twelve years.

Conclusion

It was argued in the first chapter that the challenge of development strategies in the developing countries lies not in the integration of any culture, but rather in the integration of the culture of the dominated classes. Popular Theatre has been presented as one attempt at integrating the culture of the dominated classes in the development process. Examples of Popular Theatre undertakings in Asia, Latin America, Africa, and specific case studies from Tanzania have been included to illustrate the argument.

Looking back on the Popular Theatre examples cited in this study, certain strengths and potentials in Popular Theatre as a development process which integrated the culture of the dominated classes can be observed. First is the recognition of the people's way of life as the starting point in development action. Popular Theatre begins with the grassroot community and with what its members think are the major concerns of their lives. Stage one of Popular Theatre is researching into what the community concerned conceives as their problems. The discussion and analysis of these problems by the community enables the development issues to emerge from the background of the people's own way of life. In this way, for example, the Kumba Popular Theatre workshop in Cameroon enabled the Konye people to mobilise to construct a bridge across the Mongo river, a project about which engineers and other government development agents had reached a stalemate. The Konye villagers could not previously get a bridge constructed not because they lacked the capital but because locating it at the point recommended by the engineer would slight the social and political positions of two of the three feuding groups in the village. The loss of lives of people who drowned each year, the economic losses from the difficulty in transporting cocoa and food crops across the river did not carry enough weight for the two groups to compromise their positions. Research, discussion and analysis of the different positions by the people themselves resulted in a common decision to construct the bridge at a point technically more difficult than that recommended by the engineer. For social and political reasons each group was happy to pay the extra expenses and to work together on the construction of the bridge.

All the other cases mentioned also show that it is difficult to separate the economic, social or political nature of issues. In the reality of the lives of the people concerned, these were inseparable. The problem of teenage pregnancy in Malya for example, was related to several other issues; unfavourable economic structures in the village which left the youth unemployed, the weak political organisation of the village government which did not have the strength to address the problem and finally, a breakdown of social structures previously responsible for the control of sexual behaviour. Similarly, the economic underdevelopment of Bagamoyo in Chapter 8 was not only due to the feudal economic structure but also to the belief in witchcraft which controlled much of the economic, political and social welfare of the community.

It is true that for some time now there has been a recognition of the interrelationship of economic, social and political factors in development circles, resulting in such development strategies as the integrated rural development of the 1970s or the more recent outcry for community participation as seen especially in rural water supply projects or primary health care programmes. The second contribution of Popular Theatre, though, is in approaching development from the totality of a people's way of life. Whereas other development strategies start with pre-defined agenda, say a technical rural water supply project formulated at the national level and leaving the experts to try to fit the social or so-called cultural factors into an already defined project, Popular Theatre starts with a people's way of life in general and then work out whatever development problem the people feel is of major concern.

For example, in Mkambalani the village had an acute water problem. The government water supply master plan included the Mkambalani dry taps as one of the many water systems in the region that needed rehabilitation when funds were available. But starting from the people themselves, it turned out that the problem of the dry taps was political rather than technical. And indeed, when the water eventually flowed in the Mkambalani taps there had been no technical repairs. It was the people themselves who brought out the real factors behind the water problem, factors which the technical experts either ignored or were not interested in finding out. Also in the case of Msoga what was first seen by government officials as simply laziness or unwillingness to work on the village's economic projects turned out to be deliberate resistance against dishonest political leadership.

Thirdly, the strength of Popular Theatre lies in its use of people's communication media for development. Unlike other kinds of communication for development purposes as seen in the mass media, Popular Theatre offers a communication medium where the members of the community are in control of the medium. It has been pointed out earlier how the choice of people's own theatrical forms of communication improved the people's willingness to express their views on development plans, something which radio, film, television or print has not yet effectively achieved. Indeed, Popular Theatre exposes the fact that communication tools do exist at grassroot level, outside the externally patronised media, where normally the people have no say. The neglect of this communication is part of the package of neglecting the interest of the common people. It is, as observed earlier, a deliberate step to deprive the oppressed people of the tools with which they can challenge the powers that be. Given the chance, as in the Popular Theatre cases dealt with, people do indeed come out quite strongly against the forces of their exploitation and oppression. The Mkambalani people's expression of their feelings and view on their conflict with the government officials and their winning the battle in the end offer one striking example.

This is why the question is often asked of Popular Theatre practitioners whether their work cannot be seen by the ruling powers to be subversive. A Popular Theatre venture that ends only in arousing people's emotions about their exploitation can surely result in emotional outbursts or riots. However, the challenge of Popular Theatre lies in the ability to channel the emotions and the anger into concrete and objective action to change the situation for the betterment of the people's way of life. Here one is reminded of an experience in Bangladesh where in 1983 I was participating in a Proshika organised Popular Theatre workshop among the landless peasants. During the first evening of the workshop at a Harijan village, the landless peasants put up a very involved performance expressing in very intense manner the brutality of their exploitation at the hands of the landlord. At the end of their performance almost everybody was in tears. After some minutes of tears one of the animateurs stood up and asked the people what they were going to do when they finished crying. The consequent discussion and analysis brought out the fact that crying would not do. Instead the people needed to overcome their apparent acceptance of the situation, their disunity in confronting the landlords as part of a process to free themselves from their bondage. The next stages of the workshop were, therefore, devoted to addressing those issues as well.

It should be obvious from the cases cited in this study that Popular Theatre is directed towards facilitating an articulation of problems people are facing, an exchange of ideas and viewpoints within the community with a view to finding a common ground for concrete action to solve the problems. The Msoga community, for example, was enraged by the embezzlement of the money for which they had worked hard. But the emotional outbursts which filtered into the dance and drama had to be channelled into objective decisions by the community on what action to take to bring the culprits to order and to restore the people's spirit for co-operative development action.

Popular Theatre's fourth contribution lies in it being a process for creating critical consciousness and raising the awareness of a people, as a result of which they can then take action to solve their development problems. Here Popular Theatre holds the potential for what many previous development strategies have lacked. Much has been said about the importance of awareness to a people's participation in the development process. However, a distinction has often not been made between awareness as merely possessing information about development issues or awareness in the sense of critical consciousness about the various factors of development. Most development efforts have stopped at the former. The idea has been to provide information so that people know which agricultural, health, or educational practices are desirable. A lot of material and human resources have gone into information for development. The expansion of education systems, literacy programmes, the use of posters, rural press, development programmes in the mass media are some examples. What has generally been the practice, though, is a one-way, top-down imposition of externally defined information directed at people at grassroot level. Extension workers and government and international development agents have provided the information under the assumption that it will positively influence the people for development action.

There is no question about the effectiveness of some of this information on certain development projects. The success of some mass campaigns for development programmes such as afforestation, family planning or immunization can be attributed to the effectiveness of their information networks, even where they have excluded the participation of the target audience. However, information alone is in most cases not enough to create the kind of consciousness essential for a lasting and high quality participation of people in development action. Awareness also needs to be critical so as to enable people to assess and analyse the advantages and disadvantages of their participation in development programmes. The idea is for a person to plant a tree not because of a government decree but rather because of a clear understanding that planting the tree is a process of liberation from the forces behind deforestation and their impact on his well-being. It is the absence or presence of this critical awareness which moves a person or a community to act one way or the other.

Most communication for development does not incorporate critical awareness. Several reasons account for that. One is the arrogant assumption by development agents, both national and international, that people at grassroot level are basically ignorant and incapable of comprehending development. They cannot, therefore, be expected to critically analyse or evaluate development processes, a task which is taken to be the job of development experts. What the people need is simply enough information to enable them to implement what the development agents have planned for them. Secondly, development agents would not willingly encourage a critical awareness in people for development programmes which by and large do not cater for the interests of the grassroot people.

Popular Theatre then, is an attempt to go beyond the mere provision of information and to involve people in a critical analysis of their situation. In the Murewa workshop, for example, it was important for the people to create a more critical awareness of the forces behind the loitering youth in the Murewa township. Solving that problem was not a question of simply chasing the unemployed youth from the town; rather it was a complex search for solutions to the problems of land holding, resettlement of ex-freedom-fighters and the planning of Murewa's commercial sector. The Bagamoyo people needed a critical perspective on witchcraft as it was a crucial factor in their economic exploitation by the feudal lords. As long as the fisherman was afraid of the witchcraft powers of the *mwinyi* he would be willing to settle for any pay. In fact, due to such fear, the Bagamoyo fishermen were content to accept only twenty five per cent of the fish they caught, while the rest went to the *mwinyi* who spent his time playing *bao*. Only critical awareness will free these fishermen from the grip of the feudal lords.

It is this critical awareness which then moves people to take action for development. Although this was not achieved for the Bagamoyo case, in Malya it resulted in the allocation of land to the youth. In Mkambalani it enabled the village to confront the regional and district authorities and to demand the registration of their village. In quoting these examples though, one should avoid having mechanistic notions about the achievements of Popular Theatre. The contribution of Popular Theatre to development should not be viewed only from the point of view of what development action was taken at the end of a Popular Theatre undertaking. Although it is the objective of Popular Theatre to eventually move people to take concrete action for development, Popular Theatre should be viewed as a process. It is a process in which every stage towards facilitating a meaningful participation of a people in bettering their welfare is important. Researching into the community's problems widens the people's understanding of those problems. Analysis of the problems affords them the opportunity to get another view of them as well as to contribute their own view to the causes of the problems. The result is a communal concretisation of the problems and a sharing of the interpretation of the problems by the whole community. The after-performance discussion is meant to mobilise the people into a commitment to solve their problems in a manner of their own choice.

Each stage of this process is important to development. One cannot simply single out the building of the bridge at the end as the only contribution of a Popular Theatre workshop and ignore the research, discussion, analysis, theatrical creation, and post-performance discussion that has made it possible for the people to be moved to build the bridge. The action at the end is, indeed, a desirable effect of Popular Theatre, but it ought not to be looked at in isolation from the rest of the process. The absence of concrete action at the end is not a negation of the rest of the process.

It must be noted, however, that the Popular Theatre movement also has some ideological and methodological problems and shortcomings. Some have already been pointed out above. These include the developmentalist approach, the imposition of alien forms on local communities; the low level of consciousness of some animateurs; and the lack of adequate organisational structures to support the Popular Theatre movement.

The Tanzanian Popular Theatre experience also brings up other issues demanding further attention by Popular Theatre practitioners. For example, the effective use of the indigenous forms requires some mastery of the performance skills of those forms by the animateurs to ensure their proper manipulation to carry critical content. It was mentioned above, for example, that the *Nzekule* women used their dance very effectively to air their views about the water problem, but it was difficult for the animateurs to inject an analytical and critical treatment of the content. The women who were excellent at the art of the *Nzekule* dance could not be stopped for content analysis. Probably if the animateurs were as good in the dance skills as the village women they might have managed to influence both the form and the content. This points to the need for the animateur to be well versed in both form and content.

Another problem which Popular Theatre will have to struggle with for a long time is how to confront problems whose causes and solutions are at macro level. How does a village mobilise to solve a problem caused by say flaws in national or international structures? Popular Theatre could mobilise a community to expand agricultural production but how can it empower the people to influence the price of their products considering that these are determined at the international market? Here is where the question of organisation comes in. Popular Theatre ought to be part of a broader organisation which could empower the people to confront their problems both at the micro and macro level. In Bangladesh, for example, a need was felt for a broadly based organisation of landless peasants transcending the village to fight not only one landlord but the whole feudal system. By 1984 the Proshika Aranyak Popular Theatre movement was directing its efforts towards this goal. Popular Theatre in Africa has yet to address this question. The exploited classes would need to organise themselves into a force that can confront the macro level forces of their exploitation. What kind of organisation might be suitable for that purpose requires further exploration.

These shortcomings and problems, however, ought not to be seen as indicators that Popular Theatre has failed. Instead, they should present a challenge to further efforts in improving the Popular Theatre approach. The question that remains is whether the agents of development or at least those who presently advocate the necessity of culture to development will be willing to adopt the Popular Theatre approach. The adoption of Popular Theatre will depend on one's position for or against the world's poor. Those with capitalist interests or alliances will find Popular Theatre quite contrary to their idea of development. They may, therefore, continue to ignore Popular Theatre movement. It is not surprising that in spite of the fact that the Popular Theatre movement has existed since the 1970s and has accumulated a large literature on the subject, it was ignored in the 1980s when development agents finally decided that culture was important to development programmes.

Spearheaded by UNESCO, development bodies are looking elsewhere for suggestion on how to integrate culture into development. In the typical style of the so far European controlled development strategies, European centred approaches are advocated, the most popular in this case being the use of social anthropologists and by implication anthropologists from the developed countries. Suggestions are not forthcoming which push for the need to start with the people for whom development is being planned. And since many governments are not seriously concerned about the welfare of the majority of their people, Popular Theatre does not get much attention at the national level either. Popular Theatre undertakings are normally left in the hands of a few people without the resources or the support to make it a widespread practice.

However, any government, development agent, or person committed to the meaningful development of the world's poor and the true integration of people's culture into the development process ought to take an interest in the Popular Theatre approach to culture and development. As the case of Popular Theatre in Africa vindicates, it is an attempt to approach the development of a people from the totality of their way of life.

Bibliography

AAWORD (Association of African Women for Research and Development) 1985, *Women and Rural Development in Africa*, (Proceedings of Seminar) Occasional Paper Series No. 2, Dakar.

―― 1982, "The Dakar Declaration on Another Development with Women", *Development Dialogue* 1–2, The Dag Hammarskjöld Foundation, Uppsala.

Abdalla, I. 1982, "Heterogeneity and Differentiation, The End of the Third World?", *Development Dialogue* 2, The Dag Hammarskjöld Foundation, Uppsala.

African Literature Today 1987, No. 15, "Women in African Literature Today", ed. Jones, E.D., E. Palmer and M. Jones, Africa World Press, Trenton, N.J.

African Studies by Soviet Scholars, 1984, *Ethnocultural Development of African Countries*, Social Sciences Today, Editorial Board USSR, Academy of Sciences, Moscow.

Ajayi, F. 1969, "The Place of African History and Culture in the Process of Nation Building in Africa, South of the Sahara" in Wallerstein ed., *Social Change: the Colonial Situation*, Willey, New York.

Alington, A.F. 1961, *Drama and Education*, Basil Blackwell, Oxford.

Aristotle 1927, *Poetics*, Pitman Sons, London.

Arvon, Hewi 1970, *Marxist Esthetics*, trans. from French by Helen Lane, Cornell University Press, Ithaca.

Baas, G. 1976, *Minority Theatre*, mimeo, Brown University.

Babatunde, L. 1973, "The Artist as a Creative Force in Education and Society", *Presence Africaine*, No. 86.

Biswas, K. 1983, *Political Theatre in Bengal*, mimeo, The India People's Theatre Association (IPTA).

Boesen, J. et al. ed. 1986, *Tanzania: Crisis and Struggle for Survival*, The Scandinavian Institute of African Studies, Uppsala.

Borden, E. 1968, August, "Cultural Continuity and Economic Development", *East African Journal*, Afro-Press, Nairobi.

Brookes, C., *International Popular Theatre Alliance Newsletter*, Toronto.

Bustos, N. 1982, "Interview with Nidia Bustos", *Theaterwork Magazine*, Vol. 2, No. 6, House of Print, Minnesota.

Byram, Martin et al. 1981, *The Report of the Workshop for Integrated Development*, Department of Extra Mural Studies, University of Swaziland.

Cabral, Amilcar, 1973 *Return to the Source: Selected Speeches*, Africa Information Service, New York.

―― 1980, *Unity and Struggle*, Heinemann, London.

Carlos, and Nunez, Garcia 1980, "Popular Theatre, Popular Education and Urban Community Organisation in Mexico" in Kidd, R. and N. Colleta

(eds), *Tradition for Development*, German Foundation for International Development, Berlin.
Chambulikazi, E. 1983, *Report on Msoga Popular Theatre Workshop*, (unpublished), University of Dar es Salaam.
Chepkwony, Agnes 1987, *The Role of Non-governmental Organisation in Development: A Study of the National Christian Council of Kenya (NCCK) 1963–1978*, Uppsala.
Chifunyise, S. 1978, "The formative years: An Analysis of the Development of Theatre in Zambia, 1950–70", (unpublished), Literature and Language Department, University of Zambia.
Cliffe, Lionel and John Saul 1973, *Socialism in Tanzania, Vol. 2, Policies*, East African Publishing House.
Colleta, N., and R. Kidd eds. 1980, *Tradition and Development*, German Foundation for International Development, Berlin.
Cook, C. 1917, *The Play Way*, Heinemann, London.
Courtney, R. 1968, *Play, Drama and Thought, the Intellectual Background to Drama in Education*, Drama Book Specialists, New York.
Croll, Elizabeth 1979, *Socialist Development Experience: Women in Rural Production and Reproduction in the Soviet Union, China, Cuba and Tanzania*, Institute of Development Studies, University of Sussex.
The Cultural Dimension of Development 1985, The Netherlands National Commission for UNESCO, The Hague.
Cuman, J., M. Gurerith and J. Wallocott eds. 1974, *Mass Communication and Society*, Edward Arnold, London.
Curwen, C. 1974, "Two Folk Songs from China", *The Journal of Peasant Studies*, Frank Cass and Co., Vol. 1, No. 4, July.
Debebe, E. *et al.* 1986, *Report on the Mission to Evaluate the Training of Performing Artists in Ethiopia and Tanzania for ACTPA*, mimeo, Union of African Performing Artists, Yaounde.
Dewey, John 1968, as quoted in Courtney, R., *Play, Drama and Thought*, Drama Book Specialists, New York.
Elsen, V. 1967, *The Purpose of Art*, Holt, Rinehard and Winston Inc., New York.
Etherton, M. 1982, *The Development of African Drama*, Hutchinson, London.
Eyoh, H. 1986, *From Hammocks to Bridges*, BET & Co. Pub. Ltd., Yaounde.
Faruque, A. 1987, "Empowerment in Action—Table Talk on Popular Theatre", *Adult Education Development and International Aid, Some Issues and Trends*, International Centre for Adult Education (compiled by Gunnar Rydström), Stockholm.
Fiebach, J. 1970, "The Social Function of Modern African Theatre and Brecht", *Darlite*, Vol. 4, No. 2, University of Dar es Salaam.
Fischer, E. 1959, *The Necessity of Art*, Penguin, Harmondsworth.
_____ 1969, *Art Against Ideology*, George Braziller, New York.
Foster, G.M. 1973, *Traditional Societies and Technological Change*, Harper and Row Publishers, New York.
Gargi, B. 1962, *The Theatre of India*, Theatre Art Books, New York.

Gaspar, K., "The History of the Growth and Development of Creative Dramatics in Mindanao-Sulu, The Philippines", *International Popular Theatre Alliance Newsletter*, Vol. 3.
German Adult Education Association 1982, *Adult Education and Development*, September, Special Issue, No. 19, Bonn.
Gravel, J. 1983, "Popular Theatre in Quebec", *Theaterwork Magazine*, Vol. 3, No. 5, July/August, House of Print, Minnesota.
Hall, S. 1965, *Popular Arts*, Pantheon Books, New York.
Harrap, L. 1949, *The Social Roots of the Arts*, International Publishers, New York.
Horace, F. 1934, *Art of Poetry*, trans. T. Moxon, Everyman, London.
Horfilla, N. 1984, "Theatre in Mindanao" in Tiongson ed., *The Politics of Culture. The Philippines Experience*, PETA, Manila.
Horn, A. 1984, "Public Health, Public Theatre—a Report from Southern Africa", *Medicine and Society*, X, 1–2, London.
Hussein, E. 1971, *Mashetani*, Oxford University Press, Nairobi.
_____ 1975, *The Development of Drama in East Africa*, Ph.D. thesis, Humboldt University, Berlin.
Huynh, C. 1981, *Cultural Identity and Development*, Reports/Studies, UNESCO, Paris.
Hydén, Göran 1983, *No Shortcuts to Progress*, African Dev. Management in Perspective, Heinemann, London.
Ikiara, G. 1986, "State Policy on Culture and Economic Development: the Kenya Case", Paper presented to the Regional Seminar on Culture and Economic Development, Arusha.
Ishemoi, E. 1978, *The Heroic Recitations of the Bahaya of Bukoba*, mimeo, Department of Literature, University of Dar es Salaam.
Jul-Larsen, Eyolf 1981, *The Lake is Our Shamba*, Report to NORAD about certain socio-economic aspects regarding the Lake Turkana Fishery Project, DERAP working papers, Bergen.
The Kairos Document, Challenge to the Church. A Theological Comment on the Political Crisis in South Africa, Braamfontein 1986.
Kalipeni, E. and C. Kamlongera 1987, *Popular Theatre and Health Care*, (unpublished), Chancellor College, Malawi.
Kamlongera, C. 1986, *Puppet Theatre in Malawi's Ministry of Agriculture: an Example of Extension Services in Agriculture*, paper presented to the Regional Seminar on Culture and Economic Development, Arusha.
Karibu project—Ngoma, Music and Dance in Tanzania 1974, mimeo, Ministry of Youth and Culture, Dar es Salaam.
Katoke College of Education 1984, *Mnyonge hana Haki*, (unpublished), Katoke.
Kavanagh, Robert, *Theatre and Cultural Struggle in South Africa*, Third World Books, Zed Books Ltd.
Kazooba, B. 1975, *The Art of Recitation at a Bahaya King's Court*, mimeo, University of Dar es Salaam.
Kelly, O. 1984, *Community, Art and the State: The storming citadels*, Comedia Publishing Group, London.

Kennedy, Scott 1973, *In Search of African Theatre*, Charles Scribner's Sons, New York.
Kerr, D. 1981, "An Experiment in Popular Theatre in Malawi: The University Travelling Theatre's Visit to Mbalachanda, Chancellor College" (unpublished).
Kezilahabi, E. 1981, *Kaputula la Marx*, (unpublished), Dar es Salaam.
Khan, N., and K. Bhasin 1986, "Sharing one earth", Asian South Pacific Bureau of Adult Education, *Courier Service*, No. 37.
Kidd, R. 1979, "Liberation or Domestication—Popular Theatre and Non-Formal Education in Africa", *Educational Broadcasting International*, March.
———1983, "From Outside In to Inside Out; The Benue Workshop on Theatre for Development", *Media in Education and Development*, March.
———1983, "Popular Theatre and Popular Struggle in Kenya: The Story of Kamiriithu", *Race and Class*, Vol. XXIV, 3.
———1986, *Popular Theatre: Conscientisation and Popular Organisation*, mimeo, Toronto.
Kidd, R., and M. Rashid 1984, "Theatre by the People, for the People and of the People: People's Theatre and Landless Organisation in Bangladesh", *Bulletin of Concerned Asian Scholars*, Vol. 16, No. 1.
Kidd, R., and N. Colleta eds. 1980, *Tradition and Development*, German Foundation for Development, Berlin.
Kilusang Magbukiding Pilipinas 1986, *Policy Proposals on Agriculture and Countryside Development*, Quezon city.
Kroeber, A.L. 1953, *Anthropology Today: An Encyclopedic Inventory*, University of Chicago Press, Chicago.
Leshoai, B. 1975, *Drama as a Means of Education in Africa*, Ph.D. thesis, University of Dar es Salaam.
Lihamba, Amandina 1986, *Politics and Theatre in Tanzania after the Arusha Declaration*, Ph.D. thesis, University of Leeds.
Lihamba, Amandina et al. 1976, *Harakati za Ukombozi*, Tanzania Publishing House, Dar es Salaam.
Lihamba, Amandina, and Penina Mlama 1986, *Ripoti warsha ya Sanaa kwa maendeleo ya jamii Msoga*, Chuo Kikuu Cha, (unpublished), Dar es Salaam.
Lihamba, Amandina, and Penina Mlama 1987, *Women and Communication: Popular Theatre as an Alternative Medium*, (unpublished), Association of African Women for Research on Development, Dakar.
Liyong, Taban Lo 1969, "The Role of the African Artist", in *Ghala, East African Journal*, Vol. VI, No. 1.
Liyong, Taban Lo ed. 1972, *Popular Culture of East Africa*, Longman, Nairobi.
Mair, Lucy 1984, *Anthropology and Development*, MacMillan Press, London.
Malamah, D. 1986 *Innovative Community Theatre for Integrated Rural Development in Sierra Leone: the Tellu Workshop Experience*, (unpublished) Fourah Bay.
Mao Tse-tung 1956, "Talks at the Yenan Forum on Art and Literature", *Selected Works*, International Publishers, New York.

Materego, G. 1983, *Ripoti ya washa ya Sanaa kwa maendeleo ya Jamii, Chuo Cha Sanaa Bagamoyo*, (unpublished).
Mbogo, I. 1980, *Giza Limeingia*, Tanzania Publishing House, Dar es Salaam.
Mbwana, A. 1984, *The Contribution of Modern Dance Troupes towards the Development of Traditional African Theatre*, mimeo, Department of Art, Music and Theatre, University of Dar es Salaam.
McPhee, P. 1978, "Popular Culture, Symbolism and Rural Radicalism in Nineteenth Century France", *Journal of Peasant Studies*, Vol. 5, No. 2, January.
Mda, Z. 1987, "Towards and Alternative Perspective of Development", *Union of African Performing Artists Newsletter*, Yaounde, No. 16, November.
Mlama, Penina 1973, *Music in Tanzanian Traditional Theatre*, M.A. thesis, University of Dar es Salaam.
_____ 1983, *Tanzanian Traditional Theatre as a Pedagogical Institution*, Ph.D. thesis, University of Dar es Salaam.
_____ 1984, "Theatre for Social Development: The Malya Project in Tanzania", *Third World Popular Theatre Newsletter*, International Popular Theatre Alliance, Toronto.
_____ 1986, *The Major Trends in Tanzanian Theatre Practice*, paper presented to the Janheinz Jahn Symposium, Mainz.
Mnyampala, M. 1970, *Ngonjera za Ukuta*, East African Literature Bureau, Dar es Salaam.
Morris, F. 1964, *The Heroic Recitations of the Bahima of Ankole*, Oxford University Press, Oxford.
Muhando, P. 1972, *Hatia*, East African Publishing House, Nairobi.
_____ 1983, *Nguzo Mama*, Dar es Salaam University Press, Dar es Salaam.
_____ 1984, *Lina Ubani*, Dar es Salaam University Press, Dar es Salaam.
Munslow, Barry ed. 1986, *Africa: Problems in the Transition to Socialism*, Zed Books Ltd., London.
Mwakasaka, C. 1978, *The Oral Literature of the Banyakyusa*, Kenya Literature Bureau.
Ndegwa, Philip 1985, *Africa's Development Crisis and Related International Issues*, Heinemann, Nairobi.
Ngahyoma, N. 1985, *Huka*, Tanzania Publishing House, Dar es Salaam.
Ngugi wa Thiong'o 1982 "Women in Cultural Work: the Fate of Kamiriithu People's Theatre—Kenya", *Development Dialogue*, Vol. 1–2, The Dag Hammarskjöld Foundation, Uppsala.
_____ 1983, *Barrel of a Pen: Resistance to Repression in Neo-Colonial Kenya*, New Beacon Books, London.
_____ 1986 *Decolonising the Mind*, James Currey, London.
Ngugi wa Thiong'o and Ngugi va Mirii 1982, *I Will Marry When I Want*, Heinemann, London.
Ng'wanakilala, N. 1981, *Mass Communication and Development of Socialism in Tanzania*, Tanzania Publishing House, Dar es Salaam.
Nichols, Lee ed. 1981, *Conversations with African Writers: Interview with Twenty-six African Authors*, Voice of America, Washington, DC.

Nieuwenhuijze, C. van 1983, *Culture and Development: The Prospects of an After-Thought*, Occasional Papers No. 97, Institute of Social Studies, The Hague.
Nyerere, Julius 1967, *Education for Self-Reliance*, Government Press, Dar es Salaam.
———1967, *Ujamaa*, Oxford University Press, Oxford.
———1968, *Freedom and Socialism*, Oxford University Press, Oxford.
Oke, E.A. 1984, *An Introduction to Social Anthropology*, MacMillan, London.
Olaniyan, R. ed. 1982, *African History and Culture*, Longman, Nigeria.
Omvedt, Gail 1977, "Revolutionary Music from India", *The Journal of Peasant Studies*, Frank Cass and Co., Vol. 4, No. 3, April.
Onwuejeogwu, M.A. 1975, *The Social Anthropology of Africa: An Introduction*, Heinemann, London.
Paukwa Theatre Group 1980, *Ayubu*, Urban Rural Mission Documentation Centre, Kampala.
———1986, *Mafuta*, (unpublished), Dar es Salaam.
Plato 1935, *The Republic*, trans. A.D. Lindsay, Everyman, London.
Redington, C. 1983, *Can Theatre Teach?*, Pergamon Press, Oxford.
Report on the Malya Theatre for Social Development 1982, Department of Art, Music and Theatre, Dar es Salaam.
Report on the Workshop for Training Artists in Basic Theatre Skills 1983, Department of Art, Music and Theatre, Dar es Salaam.
Ricard, Alain 1972, *Theatre and Nationalism: Wole Soyinka and Le Roi Jones*, trans. Femi Osofisan, University of Ife Press, Ile-Ife.
Rodney, Walter 1976, *How Europe Underdeveloped Africa*, Bogle-L'Ouverture, London.
Schapera, I. 1965, *Praise-Poems of Tswana Chiefs*, Oxford University Press, Oxford.
Schwitzer, P. 1980, *Theatre in Education: Four Secondary Programmes*, Methuen, London.
Shivji, Issa 1976, *Class Struggles in Tanzania*, Tanzania Publishing House, Dar es Salaam.
Songoyi, M. 1983, *Commercialisation, its Impact on Traditional Dances*, mimeo, Department of Art, Music and Theatre, University of Dar es Salaam.
Stohr, Walter and D.R. F. Taylor eds. 1981, *Development from Above or Below?*, John Wiley and Sons, New York.
Swantz, Marja-Liisa 1985, *Women in Development: A Creative Role Denied? The Case of Tanzania*, C. Hurst & Company, London.
———ed. 1985, *The Cultural Dimension of Development*, Finnish National Commission for UNESCO, Helsinki.
Swantz, Marja-Liisa, and H. Jerman eds. 1977, *Jipemoyo: Development and Culture*, No. 1, The Scandinavian Institute of African Studies, Uppsala.
Tanzania National Archives 1948, Reports of Group V Cambridge Summer Conference, TNA Secretarial file, 388/13.
Thiongson, N. 1984, *The Politics of Culture: The Philippines Experience*, PETA, Manila.

Traore, B. 1972, *The Black African Theatre and its Social Function*, trans. D. Adelugba, Ibadan University Press, Ibadan.
Ulotu, A. 1971, *Historia ya TANU*, East African Literature Bureau, Dar es Salaam.
UNESCO 1974, *Studies and Documents on Cultural Policies*, UNESCO Press, Paris.
Vansina, Jan 1965, *Oral Tradition*, Penguin, Harmondsworth.
Vazquez, A. 1973, *Art and Society: Essays in Marxist Aesthetics*, Merlin Press, London.
Vuorela, Ulla 1987, *The Women's Question and the Modes of Human Reproduction: An Analysis of a Tanzanian Village*, The Scandinavian Institute of African Studies, Uppsala.
Warren, Lee 1975, *The Theatre of Africa: an Introduction*, Prentice Hall Inc., New Jersey.
White, P. 1950, *Jungle Doctor Fables*, Paternoster Press, London.
Whiting, F. 1954, *An Introduction to the Theatre*, Harper & Row Publishers, New York.
Wizara ya Utamaduni wa Taifa na Vijana 1982, *Utamaduni Chombo cha Maendeleo*, Wizara ya Utamaduni, Dar es Salaam.
Worldview Information Foundation (WIF) 1986 *Report 1980/1986*, Colombo.